THE POLITICS OF OBEDIENCE:
THE DISCOURSE OF VOLUNTARY SERVITUDE
By Etienne de La Boetie

Introduction by
Murray N. Rothbard

Translated by
Harry Kurz

Mises Institute
518 West Magnolia Ave
Auburn, AL 36832
mises.org

ISBN: 978-1-610161-23-7

CONTENTS

THE
POLITICAL THOUGHT
OF ETIENNE
DE LA BOETIE
by Murray N. Rothbard

The Political Thought of Étienne de la Boétie

[Introduction to The Politics of Obedience: The Discourse of Voluntary Servitude by Étienne de la Boétie, written 1552-53. Translated by Harry Kurz for the edition that carried Rothbard's introduction, New York: Free Life Editions, 1975. The pagination in the footnotes refers to this 1975 edition. This online edition of Rothbard introduction 2002 (c) The Mises Institute, reprinted with the permission of the Rothbard Estate]

Étienne de La Boétie [1] has been best remembered as the great and close friend of the eminent essayist Michel de Montaigne, in one of history's most notable friendships. But he would be better remembered, as some historians have come to recognize, as one of the seminal political philosophers, not only as a founder of modern political philosophy in France but also for the timeless relevance of many of his theoretical insights.

Étienne de la Boétie was born in Sarlat, in the Perigord region of southwest France, in 1530, to an aristocratic family. His father was a royal official of the Perigord region and his mother was the sister of the president of the Bordeaux Parlement (assembly of lawyers). Orphaned at an early age, he was brought up by his uncle and namesake, the curate of Bouilbonnas, and received his law degree from the University of Orléans in 1553. His great and precocious ability earned La Boétie a royal appointment to the Bordeaux Parlement the following year, despite his being under the minimum age. There he pursued a distinguished career as

---

[1] Properly pronounced not, as might be thought, La Bo -ay- see, but rather La Bwettie (with the hard t) as it was pronounced in the perigord dialect of the region in which La Boetie lived. The definitive discussion of the proper pronunciation may be found in Paul Bonnefon, Oeuvres Completes d'Estienne de La Boetie (Bordeaux: C. Gounouilhou, and Paris: J. Rouam et Cie., 1892), pp. 385-6.

judge and diplomatic negotiator until his untimely death in 1563, at the age of thirty-two. La Boétie was also a distinguished poet and humanist, translating Xenophon and Plutarch, and being closely connected with the leading young Pleiade group of poets, including Pierre Ronsard, Jean Dorat, and Jean-Antoine de Baif.

La Boétie's great contribution to political thought was written while he was a law student at the University of Orleans, where he imbibed the spirit of free inquiry that prevailed there. In this period of questing and religious ferment, the University of Orleans was a noted center of free and untrammeled discussion. La Boétie's main teacher there was the fiery Anne du Bourg, later to become a Huguenot martyr, and burned at the stake for heresy in 1559. Du Bourg was not yet a Protestant, but was already tending in that direction, and it was no accident that this University was later to become a center of Calvinism, nor that some of La Boétie's fellow students were to become Huguenot leaders. One of these was La Boétie's best friend at the University, and Du Bourg's favorite student, Lambert Daneau. The study of law in those days was an exciting enterprise, a philosophical search for truth and fundamental principles. In the sixteenth century, writes Paul Bonnefon, "The teaching of the law was a preaching rather than an institution, a sort of search for truth, carried on by teacher and student in common, and which they feverishly undertook together, opening up an endless field for philosophic speculation."[2] It was this kind of atmosphere in the law schools of Orleans and other leading French universities in which Calvin himself, two decades earlier, had begun to develop his ideas of Protestant Reform.[3] And it was in that kind of atmosphere, as well, that lawyers were to form one of the most important centers of Calvinist strength in France.

---

[2] Bonnefon, op. cit., p. xlvi.
[3] Pierre Mesnard, L 'Essor de la Philosophie Politique Au XVIe Siecle (Paris: Boivin et Cie., 1936). p. 391.

In the ferment of his law school days at Orleans, Étienne de La Boétie composed his brief but scintillating, profound and deeply radical Discourse of Voluntary Servitude (Discours de la Servitude Volontaire).[4] The Discourse was circulated in manuscript form and never published by La Boétie. One can speculate that its radical views were an important reason for the author's with holding it from publication. It achieved a considerable fame in local Perigordian intellectual circles, however. This can be seen by the fact that Montaigne had read the essay long before he first met La Boétie as a fellow member of the Bordeaux Parlement in 1559.

The first striking thing about the Discourse is the form: La Boétie's method was speculative, abstract, deductive. This contrasts with the rather narrowly legal and historical argument of the Huguenot monarchomach writers (those sectarian writers who argued for the right of subjects to resist unjust rulers) of the 1570's and 1580's, whom La Boétie resembled in his opposition to tyranny. While the Huguenot monarchomachs, best exemplified by Francois Hotman's Franco-Gallia (1573), concentrated on grounding their arguments on real or presumed historical precedents in French laws and institutions, La Boétie's

---

[4] Having remained long in manuscript, the actual date of writing the Discourse of Voluntary Servitude remains a matter of dispute. It seems clear, however, and has been so accepted by recent authorities, that Montaigne's published story that La Boetie wrote the Discourse at the age of eighteen or even of sixteen was incorrect. Montaigne's statement, as we shall see further below, was probably part of his later .:ampalgn to guard his dead friend's reputation by dissociating him from the revolutionary Huguenots who were claiming La Boetie's pamphlet for their own. Extreme youth tended to cast the Discourse in the light of a work so youthful that the radical content was hardly to be taken seriously as the views of the author. Internal evidence as well as the erudition expressed in the work make it likely that the Discourse was written in 1552 or 1553, at the age of twenty-two, while La Boetie was at the University. See Bonnefon, op. cit., pp. xxxvi-xxxvii; Mesnard, op. cit., pp. 390-1; and Donald Frame, Montaigne: A Biography (New York: Harcourt Bracc, & World, 1965), p. 71. There is no biography of La Boetie. Closest to it is Bonnefon's "Introduction" to his Oeuvres Completes, op. cit., pp. xi-lxxxv, later reprinted as part of Paul Bonnefon, Montaigne et ses Amis (Paris: Armand Colin et Cie., 1898), I, pp. 103-224.

only historical examples were numerous illustrations of his general principles from classical antiquity, the very remoteness of which added to the timeless quality of his discourse. The later Huguenot arguments against tyranny tended to be specific and concrete, rooted in actual French institutions, and therefore their conclusions and implications were limited to promoting the specific liberties against the State of various privileged orders in French society. In contrast, the very abstraction and universality of La Boétie's thought led inexorably to radical and sweeping conclusions on the nature of tyranny, the liberty of the people, and what needed to be done to overthrow the former and secure the latter.

In his abstract, universal reasoning, his development of a true political philosophy, and his frequent references to classical antiquity, La Boétie followed the method of Renaissance writers, notably Niccolo Machiavelli. There was, however, a crucial difference: whereas Machiavelli attempted to instruct the Prince on ways of cementing his rule, La Boétie was dedicated to discussing ways to overthrow him and thus to secure the liberty of the individual. Thus, Emile Brehier makes a point of contrasting the cynical realism of Machiavelli with the "juridical idealism" of Étienne de La Boétie.[5] In fact, however, La Boétie's concentration on abstract reasoning and on the universal rights of the individual might better be characterized as foreshadowing the political thinking of the eighteenth century. As J. W. Allen writes, the Discourse was an "essay on the natural liberty, equality and fraternity of man." The essay "gave a general support to the Huguenot pamphleteers by its insistence that natural law and natural rights justified forcible resistance to tyrannous government." But the language of universal natural

---

[5] Emile Brehier, Histoire de la Philosophie, Vol. I: Moyen Age et Renaissance, cited in Mesnard, op. cit., p. 404n. Also see Joseph Banere, Estienne de La Boetie contre Nicholas Machiavel (Bordeaux, 1908), cited in ibid.

rights itself, Allen correctly adds, "served no Huguenot purpose. It served, in truth, no purpose at all at the time, though, one day, it might come to do so."[6] Or, as Harold Laski trenchantly put it: "A sense of popular right such as the friend of Montaigne depicts is, indeed, as remote from the spirit of the time as the anarchy of Herbert Spencer in an age committed to government interference."[7]

The contrast between the proto-eighteenth-century speculative natural rights approach of La Boétie, and the narrowly legalistic and concrete-historical emphasis of the Huguenot writers who reprinted and used the Discourse, has been stressed by W. F. Church. In contrast to the "legal approach" which dominated political thought in sixteenth-century France, Church writes, (purely speculative treatises, so characteristic of the eighteenth century, were all but non-existent and at their rare appearances seem oddly out of place.(Church then mentions as an example of the latter La Boétie's Discourse of Voluntary Servitude.[8]

The Discourse of Voluntary Servitude is lucidly and coherently structured around a single axiom, a single percipient insight into the nature not only of tyranny, but implicitly of the State apparatus itself. Many medieval writers had attacked tyranny, but La Boétie delves especially deeply into its nature, and into the nature of State rule itself. This fundamental insight was that every tyranny must necessarily be grounded upon general popular acceptance. In short, the bulk of the people themselves, for whatever reason, acquiesce in their own subjection. If this were not the case, no tyranny, indeed no

---

[6] J. W .Allen, A History of Political Thought in the Sixteenth Century (New York: Barnes and Noble, 1960), p. 314.
[7] Harold J. Laski, "Introduction," A Defence of Liberty Against Tyrants (Gloucester, Mass.: Peter Smith, 1963), p. 11.
[8] William Fan Church, Constitutional Thought in Sixteenth- Century France (Cambridge, Mass.: Harvard University Press, 1941), p. 13 and 13n.

governmental rule, could long endure. Hence, a government does not have to be popularly elected to enjoy general public support; for general public support is in the very nature of all governments that endure, including the most oppressive of tyrannies. The tyrant is but one person, and could scarcely command the obedience of another person, much less of an entire country, if most of the subjects did not grant their obedience by their own consent.[9]

This, then, becomes for La Boétie the central problem of political theory: why in the world do people consent to their own enslavement? La Boétie cuts to the heart of what is, or rather should be, the central problem of political philosophy: the mystery of civil obedience. Why do people, in all times and places, obey the commands of the government, which always constitutes a small minority of the society? To La Boétie the spectacle of general consent to despotism is puzzling and appalling:

> I should like merely to understand how it happens that so many men, so many villages, so many cities, so many nations, sometimes suffer under a single tyrant who has no other power than the power they give him; who is able to harm them only to the extent to which they have the

---

[9] David Hume independently discovered this principle two centuries later, and phrased it with his usual succinctness and clarity:

Nothing appears more surprising to those who consider human affairs with a philosophical eye, than the easiness with which the many are governed by the few; and the implicit submission, with which men resign their own sentiments and passions to those of their rulers. When we enquire by what means this wonder is effected, we shall find, that, as Force is always on the side of the governed, the governors have nothing to support them but opinion. It is therefore, on opinion only that government is founded; and this maxim extends to the most despotic and military governments, as well as to the most free and most popular.

David Hume, "Of the First Principles of Government," in Essays, Literary, Moral and Political.

willingness to bear with him; who could do them absolutely no injury unless they preferred to put up with him rather than contradict him. Surely a striking situation! Yet it is so common that one must grieve the more and wonder the less at the spectacle of a million men serving in wretchedness, their necks under the yoke, not constrained by a greater multitude than they...[10]

And this mass submission must be out of consent rather than simply out of fear:

> Shall we call subjection to such a leader cowardice? ... If a hundred, if a thousand endure the caprice of a single man, should we not rather say that they lack not the courage but the desire to rise against him, and that such an attitude indicates indifference rather than cowardice? When not a hundred, not a thousand men, but a hundred provinces, a thousand cities, a million men, refuse to assail a single man from whom the kindest treatment received is the infliction of serfdom and slavery, what shall we call that? Is it cowardice? ... When a thousand, a million men, a thousand cities, fail to protect themselves against the domination of one man, this cannot be called cowardly, for cowardice does not sink to such a depth. . . . What monstrous vice, then, is this which does not even deserve to be called cowardice, a vice for which no term can be found vile enough . . . ? [11]

---

[10] See p. 46 below..
[11] p. 48.

It is evident from the above passages that La Boétie is bitterly opposed to tyranny and to the public's consent to its own subjection. He makes clear also that this opposition is grounded on a theory of natural law and a natural right to liberty. In childhood, presumably because the rational faculties are not yet developed, we obey our parents; but when grown, we should follow our own reason, as free individuals. As La Boétie puts it: "If we led our lives according to the ways intended by nature and the lessons taught by her, we should be intuitively obedient to our parents; later we should adopt reason as our guide and become slaves to nobody."[12] Reason is our guide to the facts and laws of nature and to humanity's proper path, and each of us has "in our souls some native seed of reason, which, if nourished by good counsel and training, flowers into virtue, but which, on the other hand, if unable to resist the vices surrounding it, is stifled and blighted."[13] And reason, La Boétie adds, teaches us the justice of equal liberty for all. For reason shows us that nature has, among other things, granted us the common gift of voice and speech. Therefore, "there can be no further doubt that we are all naturally free," and hence it cannot be asserted that "nature has placed some of us in slavery."[14] Even animals, he points out, display a natural instinct to be free. But then, what in the world "has so, denatured man that he, the only creature really born to be free, lacks the memory of his original condition and the desire to return to it?"[15]

La Boétie's celebrated and creatively original call for civil disobedience, for mass non-violent resistance as a method for the overthrow of tyranny, stems directly from the above two premises: the fact that all rule rests on the consent of the subject masses, and the great value of natural liberty. For if tyranny

---

[12] p. 55
[13] pp. 55-56.
[14] p. 56.
[15] p. 58.

really rests on mass consent, then the obvious means for its overthrow is simply by mass withdrawal of that consent. The weight of tyranny would quickly and suddenly collapse under such a non-violent revolution. (The Tory David Hume did not, unsurprisingly, draw similar conclusions from his theory of mass consent as the basis of all governmental rule.)

Thus, after concluding that all tyranny rests on popular consent, La Boétie eloquently concludes that "obviously there is no need of fighting to overcome this single tyrant, for he is automatically defeated if the country refuses consent to its own enslavement." Tyrants need not be expropriated by force; they need only be deprived of the public's continuing supply of funds and resources. The more one yields to tyrants, La Boétie points out, the stronger and mightier they become. But if the tyrants "are simply not obeyed," they become "undone and as nothing." La Boétie then exhorts the "poor, wretched, and stupid peoples" to cast off their chains by refusing to supply the tyrant any further with the instruments of their own oppression. The tyrant, indeed, has

nothing more than the power that you confer upon him to destroy you. Where has he acquired enough eyes to spy upon you, if you do not provide them yourselves? How can he have so many arms to beat you with, if he does not borrow them from you? The feet that trample down your cities, where does he get them if they are not your own? How does he have any power over you except through you? How would he dare assail you if he had not cooperation from you?

La Boétie concludes his exhortation by assuring the masses that to overthrow the tyrant they need not act, nor shed their blood. They can do so "merely by willing to be free." In short,

Resolve to serve no more, and you are at once freed. I do not ask that you place hands upon the tyrant to topple him over, but simply that you support him no longer;

17

then you will behold him, like a great Colossus whose pedestal has been pulled away, fall of his own weight and break in pieces.[16]

It was a medieval tradition to justify tyrannicide of unjust rulers who break the divine law, but La Boétie's doctrine, though non-violent, was in the deepest sense far more radical. For while the assassination of a tyrant is simply an isolated individual act within an existing political system, mass civil disobedience, being a direct act on the part of large masses of people, is far more revolutionary in launching a transformation of the system itself. It is also more elegant and profound in theoretical terms, flowing immediately as it does from La Boétie's insight about power necessarily resting on popular consent; for then the remedy to power is simply to withdraw that consent."[17]

THE CALL for mass civil disobedience was picked up by one of the more radical of the later Huguenot pamphlets, La France Turquie (1575), which advocated an association of towns and provinces for the purpose of refusing to pay all taxes to the State.[18] But it is not surprising that among the most enthusiastic advocates of mass civil disobedience have been the anarchist thinkers, who simply extend both La Boétie's analysis and his conclusion from tyrannical rule to all governmental rule whatsoever. Prominent among the anarchist advocates of non-violent resistance have been Thoreau, Tolstoy, and Benjamin R. Tucker, all of the nineteenth century, and all, unsurprisingly, associated with the non-violent, pacifist branch of anarchism. Tolstoy, indeed, in setting forth his doctrine of non-violent

---

[16] pp.50-53.
[17] The historian Mesnard writes that this theory is "rigorous and profound," that the critics have never fully grasped its point, and that "it is the humanist solution to the problem of authority ." Mesnard, op. cit. , p. 400.
[18] See Laski, op. cit., p. 29; Allen, op. cit., p. 308.

anarchism, used a lengthy passage from the Discourse as the focal point for the development of his argument.[19] In addition, Gustav Landauer, the leading German anarchist of the early twentieth century, after becoming converted to a pacifist approach, made a rousing summary of La Boétie's Discourse of Voluntary Servitude the central core of his anarchist work, Die Revolution (1919). A leading Dutch pacifist-anarchist of the twentieth century, Barthelemy de Ligt, not only devoted several pages of his Conquest of Violence to discussion and praise of La Boétie's Discourse; he also translated it into Dutch in 1933.[20]

Several historians of anarchism have gone so far as to classify La Boétie's treatise itself as anarchist, which is incorrect since La Boétie never extended his analysis from tyrannical government to government per se.[21] But while La Boétie cannot be

---

[19] Thus, Tolstoy writes:

The situation of the oppressed should not be compared to the constraint used directly by the stronger on the weaker, or by a greater number on a smaller. Here, indeed it is the minority who oppress the majority , thanks to a lie established ages ago by clever people, in virtue of which men despoil each other. ...

Then, after a long quote from La Boetie, Tolstoy concludes,

It would seem that the workers, not gaining any advantage from the restraint that is exercised on them, should at last realize the lie in which they are living and free themselves in the simplest and easiest way: by abstaining from taking part in the violence that is only possible with their co-operation.

Leo Tolstoy, The Law of Love and the Law of Violence (New York: Rudolph Field, 1948), pp. 42-45.

Furthermore, Tolstoy's Letter to a Hindu, which played a central role in shaping Ghandi's thinking toward mass non-violent action, was heavily influenced by La Boetie. See Bartelemy de Ligt, The Conquest of Violence (New York, E.P. Dutton & Co., 1938), pp. 105-6.

[20] Etienne de La Boetie, Vrijwillige Slavernij (The Hague, 1933, edited by Bart. de Ligt). Cited in Bart. de Ligt, op. cit., p. 289. Also see ibid., pp. 104-6. On Landauer, see ibid., p. 106, and George Woodcock, Anarchism (Cleveland, Ohio: World Pub. Co., 1962), p. 432.

[21] Among those making this error was Max Nettlau, the outstanding historian of anarchism and himself an anarchist. Max Nettlau, Der Vorfruhling der Anarchie; Ihre Historische Entwicklung den Anfangen bis zum Jahre 1864 (Berlin, 1925). On this see Bert F. Hoselitz, "Publisher's Preface," in G.P. Maximoff, ed., The Political Philosophy of Bakunin (Glencoe, Dl.: The Free Press, 1953), pp. 9-10.

considered an anarchist, his sweeping strictures on tyranny and the universality of his political philosophy lend themselves easily to such an expansion. All this considerably disturbed La Boétie's biographer, Paul Bonnefon, who wrote of the Discourse:

> After having failed to distinguish legitimate from illicit authority, and having imprudently attacked even the principle of authority, La Boétie put forth a naive illusion. He seems to believe that man could live in a state of nature, without society and without government, and discovered that this situation would be filled with happiness for humanity. This dream is puerile. . . .[22]

To the acute analyst Pierre Mesnard, Bonnefon's alarm is wide of the mark; Mesnard believes that La Boétie defined tyranny as simply any exercise of personal power.[23] In doing so, La Boétie went beyond the traditional twofold definition of tyranny as either usurpation of power, or government against the "laws" (which were either defined as customary law, divine law, or the natural law for the "common good" of the people).[24] Whereas the traditional theory thus focused only on the means of

---

The first historian of anarchism, E. V. Zenker, a non-anarchist, made the same mistake. Thus, he wrote of La Boetie's Discourse, that it contained: "A glowing defence of Freedom, which goes so far that the sense of the necessity of authority disappears entirely. The opinion of La Boetie is that mankind does not need government; it is only necessary that man should really wish it, and he would find himself happy and free again, as if by magic."
E. V. Zenker, Anarchism (London: Methuen & Co., 1898), pp.15-16.

[22] Bonnefon, op. cit., "Introduction," p. xliii. In short, even Bonnefon, reacting gingerly to the radical nature and implications of La Boetie's work, classified it as anarchist.

[23] Mesnard, op. cit. , p. 395-6.

[24] On the classical and medieval concepts of tyranny, see John D. Lewis, "The Development of the Theory of Tyrannicide to 1660" in Oscar Jaszi and John D. Lewis, Against the Tyrant: The Tradition and Theory of Tyrannicide (Glencoe, Dl.: The Free Press, 1957), pp. 3-96, esp. pp. 3ff., 20ff.

the ruler's acquiring power, and the use made of that power, Mesnard points out that La Boétie's definition of tyranny went straight to the nature of power itself. Tyranny does not depend, as many of the older theorists had supposed, on illicit means of acquiring power, the tyrant need not be a usurper. As La Boétie declares, "There are three kinds of tyrants: some receive their proud position through elections by the people, others by force of arms, others by inheritance."[25] Usurpers or conquerors always act as if they are ruling a conquered country and those born to kingship "are scarcely any better, because they are nourished on the breast of tyranny, suck in with their milk the instincts of the, tyrant, and consider the people under them as their inherited serfs(. As for elected they would seem to be "more bearable," but they are always intriguing to convert the election into a hereditary despotism, and hence "surpass other tyrants ... in cruelty, because they find no other means to impose this new tyranny than by tightening control and removing their subjects so far from any notion of liberty that even if the memory of it is fresh it will soon be eradicated." In sum, La Boétie can find no choice between these three kinds of tyrants:

For although the means of coming into power differ, still the method of ruling is practically the same; those who are elected act as if they were breaking in bullocks; those who are conquerors make the people their prey; those who are heirs plan to treat them as if they were their natural slaves.[26]

Yet Mesnard's neat conclusion--that La Boétie meant simply to indict all personal power, all forms of monarchy, as being tyrannical--is inadequate.[27] In the first place, in the passage

---

[25] p. 58.

[26] pp. 58-59.

[27] Mesnard writes: "If La Boetie does not distinguish between monarchy and tyranny (as he was charged by Bonnefon), it is precisely because the two are equally illegitimate in his eyes, the first being only a special case of the second." Mesnard, op. cit., pp. 395-6. La Boetie also levels a general attack on monarchy when he questions whether monarchy

quoted above La Boétie indicts elected as well as other rulers. Moreover, he states that, "having several masters, according to the number one has, it amounts to being that many times unfortunate."[28] These are not precisely indictments of the concept of a republic, but they leave the definition of tyranny in La Boétie sufficiently vague so that one can easily press on the anarchist conclusions.

Why do people continue to give their consent to despotism? Why do they permit tyranny to continue? This is especially puzzling if tyranny (defined at least as all personal power) must rest on mass consent, and if the way to overthrow tyranny is therefore for the people to withdraw that consent. The remainder of La Boétie's treatise is devoted to this crucial problem, and his discussion here is as seminal and profound as it is in the earlier part of the work.

The establishment of tyranny, La Boétie points out, is most difficult at the outset, when it is first imposed. For generally, if given a free choice, people will vote to be free rather than to be slaves: "There can be no doubt that they would much prefer to be guided by reason itself than to be ordered about by the whims of a single man."[29] A possible exception was the voluntary choice by the Israelites to imitate other nations in choosing a king (Saul). Apart from that, tyranny can only be initially imposed by conquest or by deception. The conquest may be either by foreign armies or by an internal factional coup. The deception occurs in cases where the people, during wartime emergencies, select certain persons as dictators, thus providing the occasion for these individuals to fasten their power permanently upon the public. Once begun, however, the maintenance of tyranny is permitted

---

has any place among true commonwealths, "since it is hard to believe that there is anything of common wealth in a country where everything belongs to one master." p. 46.
[28] p. 46.
[29] p.59.

and bolstered by the insidious throes of habit, which quickly accustom the people to enslavement.

> It is true that in the beginning men submit under constraint and by force; but those who come after them obey without regret and perform willingly what their predecessors had done because they had to. This is why men born under the yoke and then nourished and reared in slavery are content, without further effort, to live in their native circumstance, unaware of any other state or right, and considering as quite natural the condition into which they are born ... the powerful influence of custom is in no respect more compelling than in this, namely, habituation to subjection.[30]

Thus, humanity's natural drive for liberty is finally overpowered by the force of custom, for the reason that native endowment, no matter how good, is dissipated unless encouraged, whereas environment always shapes us in its own way, whatever that might be in spite of nature's gifts."[31] Therefore, those who are born enslaved should be pitied and forgiven, "since they have not seen even the shadow of liberty, and being quite unaware of it, cannot perceive the evil endured through their own slavery...." While, in short, "it is truly the nature of man to be free and to wish to be so," yet a person's character "instinctively follows the tendencies that his training gives him... La Boétie concludes that "custom becomes the first reason for voluntary servitude." People will

---

[30] p. 60.
[31] p. 61.

grow accustomed to the idea that they have always been in subjection, that their fathers lived in the same way; they will think they are obliged to suffer this evil, and will persuade themselves by example and imitation of others, finally investing those who order them around with proprietary rights, based on the idea that it has always been that way.[32] [33]

Consent is also actively encouraged and engineered by the rulers; and this is another major reason for the persistence of civil obedience. Various devices are used by rulers to induce such consent. One method is by providing the masses with circuses, with entertaining diversions:

> Plays, farces, spectacles, gladiators, strange beasts, medals, pictures, and other such opiates, these were for ancient peoples the bait toward slavery, the price of their liberty, the instruments of tyranny. By these practices and enticements the ancient dictators so successfully lulled their subjects under the yoke, that the stupefied peoples, fascinated by the pastimes and vain pleasures flashed before their eyes, learned subservience as naively, but not so creditably, as little children learn to read by looking at bright picture books.[34]

---

[32] pp. 64-65.

[33] David Hume was later to write in his essay "Of the Origin of Government": "Habit soon consolidates what other principles of human I nature had imperfectly founded; and men, once accustomed to obedience, never think of departing from that path, in which they and their ancestors have constantly trod....

[34] pp. 69-70

Another method of inducing consent is purely ideological: duping the masses into believing that the tyrannical ruler is wise, just, and benevolent. Thus, La Boétie points out, the Roman emperors assumed the ancient title of Tribune of the People, because the concept had gained favor among the public as representing a guardian of their liberties. Hence the assumption of despotism under the cloak of the old liberal form. In modern times, La Boétie adds, rulers present a more sophisticated version of such propaganda, for "they never undertake an unjust policy, even one of some importance, without prefacing it with some pretty speech concerning public welfare and common good."[35] Reinforcing ideological propaganda is deliberate mystification: "The kings of the Assyrians and ... the Medes showed themselves in public as seldom as possible in order to set up a doubt in the minds of the rabble as to whether they were not in some way more than man... . " Symbols of mystery and magic were woven around the Crown, so that "by doing this they inspired their subjects with reverence and admiration.... It is pitiful to review the list of devices that early despots used to establish their tyranny; to discover how many little tricks they employed, always finding the populace conveniently gullible....[36] At times, tyrants have gone to the length of imputing themselves to the very status of divinity: "they have insisted on using religion for their own protection and, where possible, have borrowed a stray bit of divinity to bolster up their evil ways."[37] Thus, "tyrants, in order to strengthen their power, have made every effort to train their people not only in obedience and servility toward themselves, but also in adoration."[38]

---

[35] p. 71
[36] p. 72
[37] p. 73.
[38] p. 75.

At this point, La Boétie inserts his one and only reference to contemporary France. It is on its face extremely damaging, for he asserts that "our own leaders have employed in France certain similar [quasidivine] devices, such as toads, fleurs-de-lys, sacred vessels, and standards with flames of gold [oriflammes]."[39] He quickly adds that in this case he does not "wish, for my part, to be incredulous," for French kings "have always been so generous in times of peace and so valiant in time of war, that from birth they seem not to have been created by nature like many others, but even before birth to have been designated by Almighty God for the government and preservation of this kingdom."[40] In the light of the context of the work, it is impossible not to believe that the intent of this passage is satirical, and this interpretation is particularly confirmed by the passage immediately following, which asserts that "even if this were not so," he would not question the truth of these French traditions, because they have provided such a fine field for the flowering of French poetry. "Certainly I should be presumptuous," he concludes, surely ironically, "if I tried to cast slurs on our records and thus invade the realm of our poets."[41]

Specious ideology, mystery, circuses; in addition to these purely propagandistic devices, another device is used by rulers to gain the consent of their subjects: purchase by material benefits, bread as well as circuses. The distribution of this largesse to the people is also a method, and a particularly cunning one, of duping them into believing that they benefit from tyrannical rule.

---

[39] p. 74.

[40] Ibid.

[41] pp. 74-75. Bonnefon seizes the occasion to claim his subject as, deep down and in spite of his radical deviations, a good conservative Frenchman at heart: "It was not the intention of the young man to attack the established order. He formally excepts the king of France from his argument, and in terms which are stamped by deference and respect." Bonnefon, op. cit., p. xli. See also the critique of Bonnefon's misinterpretation by Mesnard, op. cit., p. 398.

They do not realize that they are in fact only receiving a small proportion of the wealth already filched from them by their rulers. Thus:

> Roman tyrants ... provided the city wards with feasts to cajole the rabble.... Tyrants would distribute largesse, a bushel of wheat, a gallon of wine, and a sesterce: and then everybody would shamelessly cry, "Long live the King!" The fools did not realize that they were merely recovering a portion of their own property, and that their ruler could not have given them what they were receiving without having first taken it from them. A man might one day be presented with a sesterce and gorge himself at the public feast, lauding Tiberius and Nero for handsome liberality, who on the morrow, would be forced to abandon his property to their avarice, his children to their lust, his very blood to the cruelty of these magnificent emperors, without offering any more resistance than a stone or a tree stump. The mob has always behaved in this way--eagerly open to bribes...[42]

And La Boétie goes on to cite the cases of the monstrous tyrannies of Nero and Julius Caesar, each of whose deaths was deeply mourned by the people because of his supposed liberality.

Here La Boétie proceeds to supplement this analysis of the purchase of consent by the public with another truly original contribution, one which Professor Lewis considers to be the most novel and important feature of his theory.[43] This is the establishment, as it were the permanent and continuing purchase,

---

[42] p. 70.

[43] Lewis, op. cit. pp. 56-57.

of a hierarchy of subordinate allies, a loyal band of retainers, praetorians and bureaucrats. La Boétie himself considers this factor "the mainspring and the secret of domination, the support and foundation of tyranny."[44] Here is a large sector of society which is not merely duped with occasional and negligible handouts from the State; here are individuals who make a handsome and permanent living out of the proceeds of despotism. Hence, their stake in despotism does not depend on illusion or habit or mystery; their stake is all too great and all too real. A hierarchy of patronage from the fruits of plunder is thus created and maintained: five or six individuals are the chief advisors and beneficiaries of the favors of the king. These half-dozen in a similar manner maintain six hundred "who profit under them," and the six hundred in their turn "maintain under them six thousand, whom they promote in rank, upon whom they confer the government of provinces or the direction of finances, in order that they may serve as instruments of avarice and cruelty, executing orders at the proper time and working such havoc all around that they could not last except under the shadow of the six hundred..."[45]

In this way does the fatal hierarchy pyramid and permeate down through the ranks of society, until "a hundred thousand, and even millions, cling to the tyrant by this cord to which they are tied." In short,

> when the point is reached, through big favors or little ones, that large profits or small are obtained under a tyrant, there are found almost as many people to whom tyranny seems advantageous as those to whom liberty would seem desirable. . . . Whenever a ruler makes himself a dictator, all the

---

[44] p. 77.
[45] p. 78.

> wicked dregs of the nation   ... all those who are
> corrupted by burning ambition or extraordinary
> avarice, these gather around him and support him in
> order to have a share in the booty and to constitute
> themselves petty chiefs under the big tyrant.[46]

Thus, the hierarchy of privilege descends from the large gainers from despotism, to the middling and small gainers, and finally down to the mass of the people who falsely think they gain from the receipt of petty favors. In this way the subjects are divided, and a great portion of them induced to cleave to the ruler, "just as, in order to split wood, one has to use a wedge of the wood itself." Of course, the train of the tyrant's retinue and soldiers suffer at their leader's hands, but they "can be led to endure evil if permitted to commit it, not against him who exploits them, but against those who like themselves submit, but are helpless." In short, in return for its own subjection, this order of subordinates is permitted to oppress the rest of the public.[47]

How is tyranny concretely to be overthrown, if it is cemented upon society by habit, privilege and propaganda? How are the people to be brought to the point where they will decide to withdraw their consent? In the first place, affirms La Boétie, not all the people will be deluded or sunk into habitual submission. There is always a more percipient, elite who will understand the reality of the situation; "there are always a few, better endowed than others, who feel the weight of the yoke and cannot restrain themselves from attempting to shake it off." These are the people who, in contrast to "the brutish mass," possess clear and far-sighted minds, and "have further trained them by study and

---

[46] pp. 78-79. John Lewis declares that "La Boetie here put his finger on one important element of tyranny which earlier writers had neglected and which contemporary writers sometimes ne- glect." Lewis, op. cit., p. 56.

[47] pp. 79-80.

learning." Such people never quite disappear from the world: "Even if liberty had entirely perished from the earth, such men would invent it."[48]

Because of the danger these educated people represent, tyrants often attempt to suppress education in their realms, and in that way those who "have preserved their love of freedom, still remain ineffective because, however numerous they may be, they are not known to one another; under the tyrant they have lost freedom of action, of speech, and almost of thought; they are alone in their aspiration."[49] Here La Boétie anticipates such modern analysts of totalitarianism as Hannah Arendt. But there is hope; for still the elite exists, and, culling examples once again from antiquity, La Boétie maintains that heroic leaders can arise who will not fail "to deliver their country from evil hands when they set about their task with a firm, whole-hearted and sincere intention."[50] The evident task, then, of this valiant and knowledgeable elite is to form the vanguard of the revolutionary resistance movement against the despot. Through a process of educating the public to the truth, they will give back to the people knowledge of the blessings of liberty and of the myths and illusions fostered by the State.

In addition to rousing the people to the truth, the opposition movement has another vital string to its bow: the unnatural lives lived by the despots and their hierarchy of favorites. For their lives are miserable and fearful and not happy. Tyrants live in constant and perpetual fear of the well-deserved hatred they know is borne them by every one of their subjects.[51] Courtiers and favorites live miserable, crawling, cringing lives every moment of which is bent on servilely fawning upon the ruler on

---

[48] p. 65.

[49] p. 66.

[50] Ibid.

[51] pp. 67-68.

30

whom they depend. Eventually, as enlightenment spreads among the public, the privileged favorites will begin to realize the true misery of their lot, for all their wealth can be seized from them at any moment should they fall out of step in the race for the favors of the king. When they "look at themselves as they really are . . . they will realize clearly that the townspeople, the peasants whom they trample under foot and treat worse than convicts or slaves ... are nevertheless, in comparison with themselves, better off and fairly free."[52]

Although he does not explicitly say so, it seems to be La Boétie's contention that the spread of enlightenment among the public will not only generate refusal of consent among the mass, but will also aid its course immeasurably by splitting off, by driving a wedge inside, a portion of the disaffected privileged bureaucracy.[53]

There is no better way to conclude a discussion of the content of La Boétie's notable Discourse of Voluntary Servitude than to note Mesnard's insight that "for La Boétie as for Machiavelli, authority can only be grounded on acceptance by the subjects: except that the one teaches the prince how to compel their acquiescence, while the other reveals to the people the power that would lie in their refusal."[54]

AFTER GRADUATING from law school, Étienne de La Boétie took up an eminent career as a royal official in Bordeaux. He never published the Discourse, and as he pursued a career in faithful service of the monarch, never a hint did he express along the lines of his earlier treatise. Certainly one of the reasons for Montaigne's stout insistence on his friend's conservatism and

---

[52] pp. 79-80. Also, pp. 79-86.

[53] See the thoughtful conclusion in Mesnard, op. cit. , p. 404. Also see Oscar Jaszi, "The Use and Abuse of Tyrannicide," in Jaszi and Lewis, op. cit. , pp. 254-5.

[54] Mesnard, op. cit., p. 400.

monarchical loyalty is that La Boétie had changed his political views by the time they met around 1559. Indeed, in late 1662, shortly before he died, La Boétie wrote but did not publish a manuscript forgotten and lost until recent years, in which he, with moderate conservatism, advised the State to punish Protestant leaders as rebels, to enforce Catholicism upon France, but also to reform the abuses of the Church moderately and respectably by the agency of the king and his Parlements. Protestants would then be forced to convert back to Catholicism or leave the country."[55]

Certainly it is far from unusual for a young university student, eagerly caught up in a burst of free inquiry, to be a fiery radical, only to settle into a comfortable and respectable conservatism once well entrenched in a career bound to the emoluments of the status quo. But there seems to be more here than that. For the very abstractness of La Boétie's argument in the Discourse, the very Renaissance-like remoteness of the discussion from the concrete problems of the France of his day, while universalizing and radicalizing the theory, also permitted La Boétie, even in his early days, to divorce theory from practice. It permitted him to be sincerely radical in the abstract while continuing to be conservative in the concrete. His almost inevitable shift of interest from the abstract to concrete problems in his busy career thereby caused his early radicalism to drop swiftly from sight as if it had never existed.[56]

But if his abstract method permitted La Boétie to abandon his radical conclusions rapidly in the concrete realm, it had an opposite effect on later readers. Its very timelessness made the work ever available to be applied concretely in a radical manner to later problems and institutions. And this was precisely the

---

[55] This was La Boetie's Memoir Concerning the Edict of January, 1562. See Frame, op. cit., pp. 72-3, 345.

[56] Mesnard., op. cit., pp. 405-6.

historical fate of La Boétie's Discourse. It was first published, albeit anonymously and incompletely, in the radical Huguenot pamphlet, Reveille-Matin des Francois (1574), probably written by Nicholas Barnaud with the collaboration of Theodore Beza.[57] The full text with the author's name appeared for the first time two years later, in a collection of radical Huguenot essays compiled by a Calvinist minister at Geneva, Simon Goulard.[58] Montaigne was furious at the essay's publication under revolutionary Huguenot auspices. He had intended to publish it himself. Now, however, not only did he refuse to do so, but he tried to refurbish La Boétie's conservative reputation by successively averring that his friend had been eighteen, and then sixteen, years old at the time of the essay's writing. For their part, however, even the Huguenots used La Boétie in gingerly fashion. "Attractive as was the spirit of La Boétie's essay," writes Harold Laski, "avowed and academic republicanism was meat too strong for the digestion of the time. Not that La Boétie was entirely without influence; but he was used as cautiously as an Anglican bishop might, in the sixties, have an interest in Darwinism."[59]

Almost completely forgotten in the more peaceful days of the first half of the seventeenth century in France, the Discourse became widely known again during the Enlightenment of the eighteenth century, through being printed as a supplement to Montaigne's essays, but was not particularly influential. Finally, and unsurprisingly, the essay found its metier in the midst of the French Revolution, when it was twice reprinted. Later the radical Abbe de Lammenais reprinted the Discourse with a "violent"

---

[57] See J.H.M. Salmon, The French Religious Wars in English Political Thought {Oxford: Clarendon Press, 1959), p. 19n.

[58] The third volume of the Memoires de L 'estat de France {1576). See Bonnefon, "Introduction," op. cit. , pp. xlix-l.

[59] Laski, op. cit. , p. 24.

preface of his own, and the same was done by another writer in 1852 to strike back at the coup d(etat of Napoleon III. And we have seen how the Discourse inspired the non-violent wing of the anarchist movement in the nineteenth and twentieth centuries. As the centuries went on, the abstract argument of the Discourse continued to exert a fascination for radicals and revolutionaries. The speculative thought of the young law student was taking posthumous revenge upon the respectable and eminent official of the Bordeaux Parlement.

LA BOEITE'S Discourse has a vital importance for the modern reader--an importance that goes beyond the sheer pleasure of reading a great and seminal work on political philosophy, or, for the libertarian, of reading the first libertarian political philosopher in the Western world. For La Boétie speaks most sharply to the problem which all libertarians-indeed, all opponents of despotism-find particularly difficult: the problem of strategy. Facing the devastating and seemingly overwhelming power of the modem State, how can a free and very different world be brought about? How in the world can we get from here to there, from a world of tyranny to a world of freedom? Precisely because of his abstract and timeless methodology, La Boétie offers vital insights into this eternal problem.

In the first place, La Boétie's insight that any State, no matter how ruthless and despotic, rests in the long run on the consent of the majority of the public, has not yet been absorbed into the consciousness of intellectuals opposed to State despotism. Notice, for example, how many anti-Communists write about Communist rule as if it were solely terror imposed from above on the angry and discontented masses. Many of the errors of American foreign policy have stemmed from the idea that the majority of the population of a country can never accept and believe in Communist ideas, which must therefore be imposed by either a small clique or by outside agents from existing

Communist countries. In modern political thought, only the free-market economist Ludwig von Mises has sufficiently stressed the fact that all governments must rest on majority consent.

Since despotic rule is against the interests of the bulk of the population, how then does this consent come about? Again, La Boétie highlights the point that this consent is engineered, largely by propaganda beamed at the populace by the rulers and their intellectual apologists. The devices-of bread and circuses, of ideological mystification-that rulers today use to gull the masses and gain their consent, remain the same as in La Boétie's days. The only difference is the enormous increase in the use of specialized intellectuals in the service of the rulers. But in this case, the primary task of opponents of modem tyranny is an educational one: to awaken the public to this process, to demystify and desanctify the State apparatus. Furthermore, La Boétie's analysis both of the engineering of consent and of the role played by bureaucrats and other economic interests that benefit from the State, highlights another critical problem which many modem opponents of statism have failed to recognize: that the problem of strategy is not simply one of educating the public about the "errors" committed by the government. For much of what the State does is not an error at all from its own point of view, but a means of maximizing its power, influence, and income. We have to realize that we are facing a mighty engine of power and economic exploitation, and there- fore that, at the very least, libertarian education of the public must include an expos6 of this exploitation, and of the economic interests and intellectual apologists who benefit from State rule. By confining themselves to analysis of alleged intellectual "errors," opponents of government intervention have rendered themselves ineffective. For one thing, they have been beaming their counter-propaganda at a public which does not have the equipment or the interest to follow the complex analyses of error, and which can therefore easily be rebamboozled by the experts in the employ of the State. Those experts, too, must be desanctified, and again La Boétie strengthens us in the necessity of such desanctification.

The libertarian theorist Lysander Spooner, writing over four hundred years after La Boétie, propounded the similar view that the supporters of government consisted largely of "dupes" and "knaves":

> The ostensible supporters of the Constitution, like the ostensible supporters of most other governments, are made up of three classes, viz.: 1. Knaves, a numerous and active class, who see in the government an instrument which they can use for their own aggrandizement or wealth. 2. Dupes- a large class, no doubt--each of whom, because he is allowed one voice out of millions in deciding what he may do with his own person and his own property, and because he is permitted to have the same voice in robbing, enslaving, and murdering others, that others have in robbing, enslaving, and murdering himself, is stupid enough to imagine that he is a "free man," a "sovereign"; that this is a "free government"; "a government of equal rights," "the best government on earth," and such like absurdities. 3. A class who have some appreciation of the evils of government, but either do not see how to get rid of them, or do not choose to so far sacrifice their private interests as to give themselves seriously and earnestly to the work of making a change.[60]

---

[60] Lysander Spooner, No Treason: The Constitution of No Authority {Colorado Springs, Co.: Ralph Myles Pub., 1973), p.18.

The prime task of education, then, is not simply abstract insight into governmental "errors" in advancing the general welfare, but debamboozling the public on the entire nature and procedures of the despotic State. In that task, La Boétie also speaks to us in his stress on the importance of a perceptive, vanguard elite of libertarian and anti-statist intellectuals. The role of this "cadre"-to grasp the essence of statism and to desanctify the State in the eyes and minds of the rest of the population(is crucial to the potential success of any movement to bring about a free society. It becomes, therefore, a prime libertarian task to discover, coalesce, nurture, and advance its cadre--a task of which all too many libertarians remain completely ignorant. For no amount of oppression or misery will lead to a successful movement for freedom unless such a cadre exists and is able to educate and rally the intellectuals and the general public.

There is also the hint in La Boétie of the importance of finding and encouraging disaffected portions of the ruling apparatus, and of stimulating them to break away and support the opposition to despotism. While this can hardly play a central role in a libertarian movement, all successful movements against State tyranny in the past have made use of such disaffection and inner conflicts, especially in their later stages of development.

La Boétie was also the first theorist to move from the emphasis on the importance of consent, to the strategic importance of toppling tyranny by leading the public to withdraw that consent. Hence, La Boétie was the first theorist of the strategy of mass, non-violent civil disobedience of State edicts and exactions. How practical such a tactic might be is difficult to say, especially since it has rarely been used. But the tactic of mass refusal to pay taxes, for example, is increasingly being employed in the United States today, albeit in a sporadic form. In December 1974 the residents of the city of Willimantic, Connecticut, assembled in a town meeting and rejected the entire city budget three times, finally forcing a tax cut of 9 percent. This is but one example of growing public revulsion against crippling taxation throughout the country.

On a different theme, La Boétie provides us with a hopeful note on the future of a free society. He points out that once the public experiences tyranny for a long time, it becomes inured, and heedless of the possibility of an alternative society. But this means that should State despotism ever be removed, it would be extremely difficult to reimpose statism. The bulwark of habit would be gone, and statism would be seen by all for the tyranny that it is. If a free society were ever to be established, then, the chances for its maintaining itself would be excellent.

More and more, if inarticulately, the public is rebelling, not only against onerous taxation but-in the age of Watergate-- against the whole, carefully nurtured mystique of government. Twenty years ago, the historian, Cecilia Kenyon, writing of the Anti-Federalist opponents of the adoption of the U.S. Constitution, chided them for being "men of little faith"-little faith, that is, in a strong central government.[61] It is hard to think of anyone having such unexamined faith in government today. In such an age as ours, thinkers like Étienne de La Boétie have become far more relevant, far more genuinely modern, than they have been for over a century.

Murray N. Rothbard

---

[61] Cecilia Kenyon, "Men of Little Faith: the Anti-Federalists on the Nature of Representative Government," William and Mary Quarterly {1955}, pp. 3-46./

THE POLITICS OF OBEDIENCE:
THE DISCOURSE OF VOLUNTARY SERVITUDE
By Etienne de La Boetie

Translated by
Harry Kurz

Publisher's Note:
This translation by Harry Kurz is based on the manuscript in the
Bibliotheque Nationale which may well have originally belonged
to Montaigne. It was first published here without Mr. Kurz's
marginal notes.
After so many years of unfortunate neglect, there is another new
edition recently published by Ralph Myles Publisher under the
title *The Will To Bondage*. Edited by William Flygare and with a
preface by James J. Martin, it presents the 1735 English
translation and the 1577 French text on facing pages.

The Politics of Obedience: *The Discourse of Voluntary Servitude*

(Part I)

I see no good in having several lords:
Let one alone be master, let one alone be king.

THESE WORDS Homer puts in the mouth of Ulysses,[1] as he addresses the people. If he had said nothing further than "I see no good in having several lords," it would have been well spoken. For the sake of logic he should have maintained that the rule of several could not be good since the power of one man alone, as soon as he acquires the title of master, becomes abusive and unreasonable. Instead he declared what seems preposterous: "Let one alone be master, let one alone be king." We must not be critical of Ulysses, who at the moment was perhaps obliged to speak these words in order to quell a mutiny in the army, for this reason, in my opinion, choosing language to meet the emergency rather than the truth. Yet, in the light of reason, it is a great misfortune to be at the beck and call of one master, for it is

---

[1] *Iliad*, Book II, Lines 204--205.---*H.K.*

41

impossible to be sure that he is going to be kind, since it is always in his power to be cruel whenever he pleases. As for having several masters, according to the number one has, it amounts to being that many times unfortunate. Although I do not wish at this time to discuss this much debated question, namely whether other types of government are preferable to monarchy,[2] still I should like to know, before casting doubt on the place that monarchy should occupy among commonwealths, whether or not it belongs to such a group, since it is hard to believe that there is anything of common wealth in a country where everything belongs to one master. This question, however, can remain for another time and would really require a separate treatment involving by its very nature all sorts of political discussion.

FOR THE PRESENT I should to understand how it happens that so many men, so many villages, so many cities, so many nations, sometimes suffer under a single tyrant who has no other power than the power they give him; who is able to harm them only to the extent to which they have the willingness to bear with him; who could do them absolutely no injury unless they preferred to put up with him rather than contradict him. Surely a striking situation! Yet it is so common that one must grieve the more and wonder the less at the spectacle of a million men serving in wretchedness, their necks under the yoke, not constrained by a greater multitude than they, but simply, it would seem, delighted and charmed by the name of one man alone whose power they need not fear, for he is evidently the one person whose qualities they cannot admire because of his inhumanity and brutality toward them. A weakness characteristic of human kind is that we often have to obey force; we have to make concessions; we ourselves cannot always be the stronger.

---

[2] Government by a single ruler. From the Greek *monos* (single) and *arkhein* (to command).---*H.K*

Therefore, when a nation is constrained by the fortune of war to serve a single clique, as happened when the city of Athens served the thirty Tyrants[3] one should not be amazed that the nation obeys, but simply be grieved by the situation; or rather, instead of being amazed or saddened, consider patiently the evil and look forward hopefully toward a happier future. Our nature is such that the common duties of human relationship occupy a great part of the course of our life. It is reasonable to love virtue, to esteem good deeds, to be grateful for good from whatever source we may receive it, and, often, to give up some of our comfort in order to increase the honor and advantage of some man whom we love and who deserves it. Therefore, if the inhabitants of a country have found some great personage who has shown rare foresight in protecting them in an emergency, rare boldness in defending them, rare solicitude in governing them, and if, from that point on, they contract the habit of obeying him and depending on him to such an extent that they grant him certain prerogatives, I fear that such a procedure is not prudent, inasmuch as they remove him from a position in which he was doing good and advance him to a dignity in which he may do evil. Certainly while he continues to manifest good will one need fear no harm from a man who seems to be generally well disposed.

But O good Lord! What strange phenomenon is this? What name shall we give it? What is the nature of this misfortune? What vice is it, or, rather, what degradation? To see an endless multitude of people not merely obeying, but driven to servility? Not ruled, but tyrannized over? These wretches have no wealth, no kin, nor wife nor children, not even life itself that they can call their own. They suffer plundering, wantonness, cruelty, not

---

[3] An autocratic council of thirty magistrates that governed Athens for eight months in 404 B.C. They exhibited such monstrous despotism that the city rose in anger and drove them forth.---*H.K.*

from an army, not from a barbarian horde, on account of whom they must shed their blood and sacrifice their lives, but from a single man; not from a Hercules nor from a Samson, but from a single little man. Too frequently this same little man is the most cowardly and effeminate in the nation, a stranger to the powder of battle and hesitant on the sands of the tournament; not only without energy to direct men by force, but with hardly enough virility to bed with a common woman! Shall we call subjection to such a leader cowardice? Shall we say that those who serve him are cowardly and faint-hearted? If two, if three, if four, do not defend themselves from the one, we might call that circumstance surprising but nevertheless conceivable. In such a case one might be justified in suspecting a lack of courage. But if a hundred, if a thousand endure the caprice of a single man, should we not rather say that they lack not the courage but the desire to rise against him, and that such an attitude indicates indifference rather than cowardice? When not a hundred, not a thousand men, but a hundred provinces, a thousand cities, a million men, refuse to assail a single man from whom the kindest treatment received is the infliction of serfdom and slavery, what shall we call that? Is it cowardice? Of course there is in every vice inevitably some limit beyond which one cannot go. Two, possibly ten, may fear one; but when a thousand, a million men, a thousand cities, fail to protect themselves against the domination of one man, this cannot be called cowardly, for cowardice does not sink to such a depth, any more than valor can be termed the effort of one individual to scale a fortress, to attack an army, or to conquer a kingdom. What monstrous vice, then, is this which does not even deserve to be called cowardice, a vice for which no term can be found vile enough, which nature herself disavows and our tongues refuse to name?

Place on one side fifty thousand armed men, and on the other the same number; let them join in battle, one side fighting to retain its liberty, the other to take it away; to which would you, at a guess, promise victory? Which men do you think would march more gallantly to combat---those who anticipate as a reward for their suffering the maintenance of their freedom, or those who cannot expect any other prize for the blows exchanged than the enslavement of others? One side will have before its eyes the blessings of the past and the hope of similar joy in the future; their thoughts will dwell less on the comparatively brief pain of battle than on what they may have to endure forever, they, their children, and all their posterity. The other side has nothing to inspire it with courage except the weak urge of greed, which fades before danger and which can never be so keen, it seems to me, that it will not be dismayed by the least drop of blood from wounds. Consider the justly famous battles of Miltiades,[4] Leonidas,[5] Themistocles,[6] still fresh today in recorded history and in the minds of men as if they had occurred but yesterday, battles fought in Greece for the welfare of the Greeks and as an example to the world. What power do you think gave to such a mere handful of men not the strength but the courage to withstand the attack of a fleet so vast that even the seas were burdened, and to defeat the armies of so many nations, armies so immense that their officers alone outnumbered the entire Greek force? What was it but the fact that in those glorious days this struggle represented not so much a fight of Greeks against Persians as a victory of liberty over domination, of freedom over greed?

.It amazes us to hear accounts of the valor that liberty arouses in the hearts of those who defend it; but who could believe reports of what goes on every day among the inhabitants of some

---

[4] Athenian general, died 489 B.C. Some of his battles: expedition against Scythians; Lemnos; Imbros; Marathon, where Darius the Pemian was defeated. ---*H.K.*

[5] King of Sparta, died at Thermopolae in 480 B.C., defending the pass with three hundred loyal Spartans against Xerxes. ---*H.K.*

[6] Athenian statesman and general, died 460 B.C. Some of his battles: expedition against Aegean Isles; victory over Persians under Xerxes at Salamis. ---*H.K.*

countries, who could really believe that one man alone may mistreat a hundred thousand and deprive them of their liberty? Who would credit such a report if he merely heard it, without being present to witness the event? And if this condition occurred only in distant lands and were reported to us, which one among us would not assume the tale to be imagined or invented, and not really true? Obviously there is no need of fighting to overcome this single tyrant, for he is automatically defeated if the country refuses consent to its own enslavement: it is not necessary to deprive him of anything, but simply to give him nothing; there is no need that the country make an effort to do anything for itself provided it does nothing against itself. It is therefore the inhabitants themselves who permit, or, rather, bring about, their own subjection, since by ceasing to submit they would put an end to their servitude. A people enslaves itself, cuts its own throat, when, having a choice between being vassals and being free men, it deserts its liberties and takes on the yoke, gives consent to its own misery, or, rather, apparently welcomes it. If it cost the people anything to recover its freedom, I should not urge action to this end, although there is nothing a human should hold more dear than the restoration of his own natural right, to change himself from a beast of burden back to a man, so to speak. I do not demand of him so much boldness; let him prefer the doubtful security of living wretchedly to the uncertain hope of living as he pleases. What then? If in order to have liberty nothing more is needed than to long for it, if only a simple act of the will is necessary, is there any nation in the world that considers a single wish too high a price to pay in order to recover rights which it ought to be ready to redeem at the cost of its blood, rights such that their loss must bring all men of honor to the point of feeling life to be unendurable and death itself a deliverance?

Everyone knows that the fire from a little spark will increase and blaze ever higher as long as it finds wood to burn; yet without being quenched by water, but merely by finding no more fuel to feed on, it consumes itself, dies down, and is no longer a flame. Similarly, the more tyrants pillage, the more they crave, the more they ruin and destroy; the more one yields to them, and obeys them, by that much do they become mightier and more formidable, the readier to annihilate and destroy. But if not one thing is yielded to them, if, without any violence they are simply not obeyed, they become naked and undone and as nothing, just as, when the root receives no nourishment, the branch withers and dies.

To achieve the good that they desire, the bold do not fear danger; the intelligent do not refuse to undergo suffering. It is the stupid and cowardly who are neither able to endure hardship nor to vindicate their rights; they stop at merely longing for them, and lose through timidity the valor roused by the effort to claim their rights, although the desire to enjoy them still remains as part of their nature. A longing common to both the wise and the foolish, to brave men and to cowards, is this longing for all those things which, when acquired, would make them happy and contented. Yet one element appears to be lacking. I do not know how it happens that nature fails to place within the hearts of men a burning desire for liberty, a blessing so great and so desirable that when it is lost all evils follow thereafter, and even the blessings that remain lose taste and savor because of their corruption by servitude. Liberty is the only joy upon which men do not seem to insist; for surely if they really wanted it they would receive it. Apparently they refuse this wonderful privilege because it is so easily acquired.

Poor, wretched, and stupid peoples, nations determined on your own misfortune and blind to your own good! You let yourselves be deprived before your own eyes of the best part of your revenues; your fields are plundered, your homes robbed, your family heirlooms taken away. You live in such a way that you cannot claim a single thing as your own; and it would seem that you consider yourselves lucky to be loaned your property, your families, and your very lives. All this havoc, this misfortune, this ruin, descends upon you not from alien foes, but from the one enemy whom you yourselves render as powerful as he is, for whom you go bravely to war, for whose greatness you do not refuse to offer your own bodies unto death. He who thus domineers over you has only two eyes, only two hands, only one body, no more than is possessed by the least man among the infinite numbers dwelling in your cities; he has indeed nothing more than the power that you confer upon him to destroy you. Where has he acquired enough eyes to spy upon you, if you do not provide them yourselves? How can he have so many arms to beat you with, if he does not borrow them from you? The feet that trample down your cities, where does he get them if they are not your own? How does he have any power over you except through you? How would he dare assail you if he had no cooperation from you? What could he do to you if you yourselves did not connive with the thief who plunders you, if you were not accomplices of the murderer who kills you, if you were not traitors to yourselves? You sow your crops in order that he may ravage them, you install and furnish your homes to give him goods to pillage; you rear your daughters that he may gratify his lust; you bring up your children in order that he may confer upon them the greatest privilege he knows---to be led into his battles, to be delivered to butchery, to be made the servants of his greed and the instruments of his vengeance; you yield your bodies unto hard labor in order that he may indulge in his delights and wallow in his filthy pleasures; you weaken yourselves in order to make him the stronger and the mightier to hold you in check. From all these indignities, such as the very beasts of the field would not endure, you can deliver yourselves if you try, not by taking action, but merely by willing to be free. Resolve to serve no more, and you are at once freed. I do not ask that you place hands upon the tyrant to topple him over, but simply that you support him no longer; then you will behold him, like a great Colossus whose pedestal has been pulled away, fall of his own weight and break into pieces?

(Part II)

DOCTORS ARE NO DOUBT CORRECT in warning us not to touch incurable wounds; and I am presumably taking chances in preaching as I do to a people which has long lost all sensitivity and, no longer conscious of its infirmity, is plainly suffering from mortal illness. Let us therefore understand by logic, if we can, how it happens that this obstinate willingness to submit has become so deeply rooted in a nation that the very love of liberty now seems no longer natural..

In the first place, all would agree that, if we led our lives according to the ways intended by nature and the lessons taught by her, we should be intuitively obedient to our parents; later we should adopt reason as our guide and become slaves to nobody. Concerning the obedience given instinctively to one's father and mother, we are in agreement, each one admitting himself to be a model. As to whether reason is born with us or not, that is a question loudly discussed by academicians and treated by all schools of philosophers. For the present I think I do not err in stating that there is in our souls some native seed of reason, which, if nourished by good counsel and training, flowers into virtue, but which, on the other hand, if unable to resist the vices surrounding it, is stifled and blighted. Yet surely if there is anything in this world clear and obvious, to which one cannot close one's eyes, it is the fact that nature, handmaiden of God, governess of men, has cast us all in the same mold in order that we may behold in one another companions, or rather brothers. If in distributing her gifts nature has favored some more than others with respect to body or spirit, she has nevertheless not planned to place us within this world as if it were a field of battle, and has not endowed the stronger or the cleverer in order that they may act like armed brigands in a forest and attack the weaker. One should rather conclude that in distributing larger shares to some and smaller shares to others, nature has intended to give occasion for brotherly love to become manifest, some of us having the strength to give help to others who are in need of it. Hence, since this kind mother has given us the whole world as a dwelling place, has lodged us in the same house, has fashioned us according to the same model so that in beholding one another we might almost recognize ourselves; since she has bestowed upon us all the great gift of voice and speech for fraternal relationship, thus achieving by the common and mutual statement of our thoughts a communion of our wills; and since she has tried in every way to narrow and tighten the bond of our union and kinship; since she has revealed in every possible manner her intention, not so much to associate us as to make us one organic whole, there can be no further doubt that we are all naturally free, inasmuch as we are all comrades. Accordingly it should not enter the mind of anyone that nature has placed some of us in slavery, since she has actually created us all in one likeness..

Therefore it is fruitless to argue whether or not liberty is natural, since none can be held in slavery without being wronged, and in a world governed by a nature, which is reasonable, there is nothing so contrary as an injustice. Since freedom is our natural state, we are not only in possession of it but have the urge to defend it. Now, if perchance some cast a doubt on this conclusion and are so corrupted that they are not able to recognize their rights and inborn tendencies, I shall have to do them the honor that is properly theirs and place, so to speak, brute beasts in the pulpit to throw light on their nature and condition, The very beasts, God help me! if men are not too deaf, cry out to them, "Long live Liberty!" Many among them die as soon as captured: just as the fish loses life as soon as he leaves the water, so do these creatures close their eyes upon the light and have no desire to survive the loss of their natural freedom. If the animals were to constitute their kingdom by rank, their nobility would be chosen from this type. Others, from the largest to the smallest, when captured put up such a strong resistance by means of claws, horns, beak, and paws, that they show clearly enough how they cling to what they are losing; afterwards in captivity they manifest by so many evident signs their awareness of their misfortune, that it is easy to see they are languishing rather than living, and continue their existence---more in lamentation of their lost freedom than in enjoyment of their servitude. What else can explain the behavior of the elephant who, after defending himself to the last ounce of his strength and knowing himself on the point of being taken, dashes his jaws against the trees and breaks his tusks, thus manifesting his longing to remain free as he has been and proving his wit and ability to buy off the huntsmen in the hope that through the sacrifice of his tusks he will be permitted to offer his ivory as a ransom for his liberty? We feed the horse from birth in order to train him to do our bidding. Yet he is tamed with such difficulty that when we begin to break him in he bites the bit, he rears at the touch of the spur, as if to reveal his instinct and show by his actions that, if he obeys, he does so not of his own free will but under constraint. What more can we say?

Even the oxen under the weight of the yoke

complain,
And the birds in their cage lament,

as I expressed it some time ago, toying with our French poesy. For I shall not hesitate in writing to you, O Longa, to introduce some of my verses, which I never read to you because of your obvious encouragement which is quite likely to make me conceited. And now, since all beings, because they feel, suffer misery in subjection and long for liberty; since the very beasts, although made for the service of man, cannot become accustomed to control without protest, what evil chance has so denatured man that he, the only creature really born to be free, lacks the memory of his original condition and the desire to return to it?

There are three kinds of tyrants; some receive their proud position through elections by the people, others by force of arms, others by inheritance. Those who have acquired power by means of war act in such wise that it is evident they rule over a conquered country. Those who are born to kingship are scarcely any better, because they are nourished on the breast of tyranny, suck in with their milk the instincts of the tyrant, and consider the people under them as their inherited serfs; and according to their individual disposition, miserly or prodigal, they treat their kingdom as their property. He who has received the state from the people, however, ought to be, it seems to me, more bearable and would be so, I think, were it not for the fact that as soon as he sees himself higher than the others, flattered by that quality which we call grandeur, he plans never to relinquish his position. Such a man usually determines to pass on to his children the authority that the people have conferred upon him; and once his heirs have taken this attitude, strange it is how far they surpass other tyrants in all sorts of vices, and especially in cruelty, because they find no other means to impose this new tyranny than by tightening control and removing their subjects so far from any notion of liberty that even if the memory of it is fresh it will soon be eradicated. Yet, to speak accurately, I do perceive that there is some difference among these three types of tyranny, but as for stating a preference, I cannot grant there is any. For although the means of coming into power differ, still the method of ruling is practically the same; those who are elected act as if they were breaking in bullocks; those who are conquerors make the people their prey; those who are heirs plan to treat them as if they were their natural slaves.

In connection with this, let us imagine some newborn individuals, neither acquainted with slavery nor desirous of liberty, ignorant indeed of the very words. If they were permitted to choose between being slaves and free men, to which would they give their vote? There can be no doubt that they would much prefer to be guided by reason itself than to be ordered about by the whims of a single man. The only possible exception might be the Israelites who, without any compulsion or need, appointed a tyrant.[7] I can never read their history without becoming angered and even inhuman enough to find satisfaction in the many evils that befell them on this account. But certainly all men, as long as they remain men, before letting themselves become enslaved must either be driven by force or led into it by deception; conquered by foreign armies, as were Sparta and Athens by the forces of Alexander[8] or by political factions, as when at an earlier period the control of Athens had passed into the hands of Pisistrates.[9] When they lose their liberty through deceit they are not so often betrayed by others as misled by themselves. This was the case with the people of Syracuse, chief

---

[7] The reference is to Saul anointed by Samuel.---*H.K.*

[8] Alexander the Macedonian became the acknowledged master of all Hellenes at the Assembly of Corinth, 335 B.C.---*H.K.*

[9] Athenian tyrant, died 627 B.C. He used ruse and bluster to control the city and was obliged to flee several times.---*H.K.*

....

city of Sicily when, in the throes of war and heedlessly planning only for the present danger, they promoted Denis,[10] their first tyrant, by entrusting to him the command of the army, without realizing that they had given him such power that on his victorious return this worthy man would behave as if he had vanquished not his enemies but his compatriots, transforming himself from captain to king, and then from king to tyrant.[11].

It is incredible how as soon as a people becomes subject, it promptly falls into such complete forgetfulness of its freedom that it can hardly be roused to the point of regaining it, obeying so easily and so willingly that one is led to say, on beholding such a situation, that this people has not so much lost its liberty as won its enslavement. It is true that in the beginning men submit under constraint and by force; but those who come after them obey without regret and perform willingly what their predecessors had done because they had to. This is why men born under the yoke and then nourished and reared in slavery are content, without further effort, to live in their native circumstance, unaware of any other state or right, and considering as quite natural the condition into which they were born. There is, however, no heir so spendthrift or indifferent that he does not sometimes scan the account books of his father in order to see if he is enjoying all the privileges of his legacy or whether, perchance, his rights and those of his predecessor have not been encroached upon. Nevertheless it is clear enough that the powerful influence of custom is in no respect more compelling than in this, namely, habituation to subjection. It is said that Mithridates[12] trained himself to drink poison. Like him

---

[10] Denis or Dionysius, tyrant of Syracuse, died in 367 B.C. Of lowly birth, this dictator imposed himself by plottings, putsches, and purges. The danger from which he saved his city was the invasion by the Carthaginians. ---H.K.

[11] Dionysius seized power in Syraeuse in 405 B.C. ---M.N.R.

[12] Mithridates (c. 135--63 B.C.) was next to Hannibal the most dreaded and potent enemy of Roman power. The reference in the text is to his youth when he spent some years in

we learn to swallow, and not to find bitter, the venom of servitude. It cannot be denied that nature is influential in shaping us to her will and making us reveal our rich or meager endowment; yet it must be admitted that she has less power over us than custom, for the reason that native endowment, no matter how good, is dissipated unless encouraged, whereas environment always shapes us in its own way, whatever that may be, in spite of nature's gifts. The good seed that nature plants in us is so slight and so slippery that it cannot withstand the least harm from wrong nourishment; it flourishes less easily, becomes spoiled, withers, and comes to nothing. Fruit trees retain their own particular quality if permitted to grow undisturbed, but lose it promptly and bear strange fruit not their own when ingrafted. Every herb has its peculiar characteristics, its virtues and properties; yet frost, weather, soil, or the gardener's hand increase or diminish its strength; the plant seen one spot cannot be recognized in another..

Whoever could have observed the early Venetians, a handful of people living so freely that the most wicked among them would not wish to be king over them, so born and trained that they would not vie with one another except as to which one could give the best counsel and nurture their liberty most carefully, so instructed and developed from their cradles that they would not exchange for all the other delights of the world an iota of their freedom; who, I say, familiar with the original nature of such a people, could visit today the territories of the man known as the Great Doge,[13] and there contemplate with composure a people unwilling to live except to serve him, and maintaining his power at the cost of their lives? Who would

---

retirement hardening himself and immunizing himself against poison. In his old age, defeated by Pompey, betrayed by his own son, he tried poison and Finally had to resort to the dagger of a friendly Gaul. (Pliny, *Natural History*, XXIV, 2.)---*H.K.*

[13] The ruler of Venice.---*M.N.R.*

believe that these two groups of people had an identical origin? Would one not rather conclude that upon leaving a city of men he had chanced upon a menagerie of beasts? Lycurgus,[14] the lawgiver of Sparta, is reported to have reared two dogs of the same litter by fattening one in the kitchen and training the other in the fields to the sound of the bugle and the horn, thereby to demonstrate to the Lacedaemonians that men, too, develop according to their early habits. He set the two dogs in the open market place, and between them he placed a bowl of soup and a hare. One ran to the bowl of soup, the other to the hare; yet they were, as he maintained, born brothers of the same parents. In such manner did this leader, by his laws and customs, shape and instruct the Spartans so well that any one of them would sooner have died than acknowledge any sovereign other than law and reason.

It gives me pleasure to recall a conversation of the olden time between one of the favorites of Xerxes, the great king of Persia, and two Lacedaemonians. When Xerxes equipped his great army to conquer Greece, he sent his ambassadors into the Greek cities to ask for water and earth. That was the procedure the Persians adopted in summoning the cities to surrender. Neither to Athens nor to Sparta, however, did he dispatch such messengers, because those who had been sent there by Darius his father had been thrown, by the Athenians and Spartans, some into ditches and others into wells, with the invitation to help themselves freely there to water and soil to take back to their prince. Those Greeks could not permit even the slightest suggestion of encroachment upon their liberty. The Spartans suspected, nevertheless, that they had incurred the wrath of the gods by their action, and especially the wrath of Talthybios, the god of

---

[14] A half-legendary figure concerning whose life Plutarch admits there is much obscurity. He bequeathed to his land a rigid code regulating land, assembly, education, with the individual subordinate to the state.---*H.K.*

the heralds; in order to appease him they decided to send Xerxes two of their citizens in atonement for the cruel death inflicted upon the ambassadors of his father. Two Spartans, one named Sperte and the other Bulis, volunteered to offer themselves as a sacrifice. So they departed, and on the way they came to the palace of the Persian named Hydarnes, lieutenant of the king in all the Asiatic cities situated on the sea coasts. He received them with great honor, feasted them, and then, speaking of one thing and another, he asked them why they refused so obdurately his king's friendship. "Consider well, O Spartans," said he, "and realize by my example that the king knows how to honor those who are worthy, and believe that if you were his men he would do the same for you; if you belonged to him and he had known you, there is not one among you who might not be the lord of some Greek city."

"By such words, Hydarnes, you give us no good counsel," replied the Lacedaemonians, "because you have experienced merely the advantage of which you speak; you do not know the privilege we enjoy. You have the honor of the king's favor; but you know nothing about liberty, what relish it has and how sweet it is. For if you had any knowledge of it, you yourself would advise us to defend it, not with lance and shield, but with our very teeth and nails."

Only Spartans could give such an answer, and surely both of them spoke as they had been trained. It was impossible for the Persian to regret liberty, not having known it, nor for the Lacedaemonians to find subjection acceptable after having enjoyed   freedom.

Cato the Utican, while still a child under the rod, could come and go in the house of Sylla the despot. Because of the place and family of his origin and because he and Sylla were close relatives, the door was never closed to him. He always had his teacher with him when he went there, as was the custom for children of noble birth. He noticed that in the house of Sylla, in the dictator's presence or at his command, some men were imprisoned and others sentenced; one was banished, another was strangled; one demanded the goods of another citizen, another his head; in short, all went there, not as to the house of a city magistrate but as to the people's tyrant, and this was therefore not a court of justice, but rather a resort of tyranny. Whereupon the young lad said to his teacher, "Why don't you give me a dagger? I will hide it under my robe. I often go into Sylla's room before he is risen, and my arm is strong enough to rid the city of him." There is a speech truly characteristic of Cato; it was a true beginning of this hero so worthy of his end. And should one not mention his name or his country, but state merely the fact as it is, the episode itself would speak eloquently, and anyone would divine that he was a Roman born in Rome at the time when she was free.

And why all this? Certainly not because I believe that the land or the region has anything to do with it, for in any place and in any climate subjection is bitter and to be free is pleasant; but merely because I am of the opinion that one should pity those who, at birth, arrive with the yoke upon their necks. We should exonerate and forgive them, since they have not seen even the shadow of liberty, and, being quite unaware of it, cannot perceive the evil endured through their own slavery. If there were actually a country like that of the Cimmerians mentioned by Homer,[15] where the sun shines otherwise than on our own, shedding its radiance steadily for six successive months and then leaving humanity to drowse in obscurity until it returns at the end of another half-year, should we be surprised to learn that those born during this long night do grow so accustomed to their native darkness that unless they were told about the sun they

---

[15] *Odyssey.* Book II, Lines 14--19. The Cimmerians were a barbarian people active north of the Black Sea in the eighth and seventh centuries B.C., and gave their name to Crimea.---*M.N.R.*

would have no desire to see the light? One never pines for what he has never known; longing comes only after enjoyment and constitutes, amidst the experience of sorrow, the memory of past joy. It is truly the nature of man to be free and to wish to be so, yet his character is such that he instinctively follows the tendencies that his training gives him.

Let us therefore admit that all those things to which he is trained and accustomed seem natural to man and that only that is truly native to him which he receives with his primitive, untrained individuality. Thus custom becomes the first reason for voluntary servitude. Men are like handsome race horses who first bite the bit and later like it, and rearing under the saddle a while soon learn to enjoy displaying their harness and prance proudly beneath their trappings. Similarly men will grow accustomed to the idea that they have always been in subjection, that their fathers lived in the same way; they will think they are obliged to suffer this evil, and will persuade themselves by example and imitation of others, finally investing those who order them around with proprietary rights, based on the idea that it has always been that way.

There are always a few, better endowed than others, who feel the weight of the yoke and cannot restrain themselves from attempting to shake it off: these are the men who never become tamed under subjection and who always, like Ulysses on land and sea constantly seeking the smoke of his chimney, cannot prevent themselves from peering about for their natural privileges and from remembering their ancestors and their former ways. These are in fact the men who, possessed of clear minds and far-sighted spirit, are not satisfied, like the brutish mass, to see only what is at their feet, but rather look about them, behind and before, and even recall the things of the past in order to judge those of the future, and compare both with their present condition. These are the ones who, having good minds of their own, have further trained them by study and learning. Even if

60

liberty had entirely perished from the earth, such men would invent it. For them slavery has no satisfactions, no matter how well disguised.

The Grand Turk[16] was well aware that books and teaching more than anything else give men the sense to comprehend their own nature and to detest tyranny. I understand that in his territory there are few educated people, for he does not want many. On account of this restriction, men of strong zeal and devotion, who in spite of the passing of time have preserved their love of freedom, still remain ineffective because, however numerous they may be, they are not known to one another; under the tyrant they have lost freedom of action, of speech, and almost of thought; they are alone in their aspiration. Indeed Momus, god of mockery, was not merely joking when he found this to criticize in the man fashioned by Vulcan, namely, that the maker had not set a little window in his creature's heart to render his thoughts visible. It is reported that Brutus, Cassius, and Casca, on undertaking to free Rome, and for that matter the whole world, refused to include in their band Cicero, that great enthusiast for the public welfare if ever there was one, because they considered his heart too timid for such a lofty deed; they trusted his willingness but they were none too sure of his courage. Yet whoever studies the deeds of earlier days and the annals of antiquity will find practically no instance of heroes who failed to deliver their country from evil hands when they set about their task with a firm, whole-hearted, and sincere intention. Liberty, as if to reveal her nature, seems to have given them new strength. Harmodios and Aristogiton, Thrasybulus, Brutus the Elder, Valerianus, and Dion achieved successfully what they planned virtuously: for hardly ever does good fortune fail a strong will. Brutus the Younger and Cassius were successful in eliminating servitude, and although they perished in their attempt

---

[16] The Ottoman Sultan of Constantinople was often called the Grand Turk.---*M.N.R*

to restore liberty, they did not die miserably (what blasphemy it would be to say there was anything miserable about these men, either in their death or in their living!).[17] Their loss worked great harm, everlasting misfortune, and complete destruction of the Republic, which appears to have been buried with them. Other and later undertakings against the Roman emperors were merely plottings of ambitious people, who deserve no pity for the misfortunes that overtook them, for it is evident that they sought not to destroy, but merely to usurp the crown, scheming to drive away the tyrant, but to retain tyranny. For myself, I could not wish such men to propser and I am glad they have shown by their example that the sacred name of Liberty must never be used to cover a false enterprise.

But to come back to the thread of our discourse, which I have practically lost: the essential reason why men take orders willingly is that they are born serfs and are reared as such. From this cause there follows another result, namely that people easily become cowardly and submissive under tyrants. For this observation I am deeply grateful to Hippocrates, the renowned father of medicine, who noted and reported it in a treatise of his entitled Concerning Diseases. This famous man was certainly endowed with a great heart and proved it clearly by his reply to the Great King, who wanted to attach him to his person by means of special privileges and large gifts. Hippocrates answered frankly that it would be a weight on his conscience to make use of his science for the cure of barbarians who wished to slay his fellow Greeks, or to serve faithfully by his skill anyone who undertook to enslave Greece. The letter he sent the king can still be read among his other works and will forever testify to his great heart and noble character.

---

[17] Brutus and Cassias helped to assassinate Julius Caesar in 44 B.C. They committed suicide after being defeated by Marcus Antonius at the Battles of Philippi in 42 B.C. — *M.N.R.*

.By this time it should be evident that liberty once lost, valor also perishes. A subject people shows neither gladness nor eagerness in combat: its men march sullenly to danger almost as if in bonds, and stultified; they do not feel throbbing within them that eagerness for liberty which engenders scorn of peril and imparts readiness to acquire honor and glory by a brave death amidst one's comrades. Among free men there is competition as to who will do most, each for the common good, each by himself, all expecting to share in the misfortunes of defeat, or in the benefits of victory; but an enslaved people loses in addition to this warlike courage, all signs of enthusiasm, for their hearts are degraded, submissive, and incapable of any great deed. Tyrants are well aware of this, and, in order to degrade their subjects further, encourage them to assume this attitude and make it instinctive.

Xenophon, grave historian of first rank among the Greeks, wrote a book in which he makes Simonides speak with Hieron, Tyrant of Syracuse, concerning the anxieties of the tyrant. This book is full of fine and serious remonstrances, which in my opinion are as persuasive as words can be. Would to God that all despots who have ever lived might have kept it before their eyes and used it as a mirror! I cannot believe they would have failed to recognize their warts and to have conceived some shame for their blotches. In this treatise is explained the torment in which tyrants find themselves when obliged to fear everyone because they do evil unto every man. Among other things we find the statement that bad kings employ foreigners in their wars and pay them, not daring to entrust weapons in the hands of their own people, whom they have wronged. (There have been good kings who have used mercenaries from foreign nations, even among the French, although more so formerly than today, but with the quite different purpose of preserving their own people, considering as nothing the loss of money in the effort to spare French lives. That is, I believe, what Scipio the great African meant when he said he would rather save one citizen than defeat a hundred enemies.) For it is plainly evident that the dictator does not consider his power firmly established until he has reached the point where there is no man under him who is of any worth. Therefore there may be justly applied to him the reproach to the master of the elephants made by Thrason and reported by Terence:

> Are you indeed so proud
> Because you command wild beasts?

This method tyrants use of stultifying their subjects cannot be more clearly observed than in what Cyrus did with the Lydians after he had taken Sardis, their chief city, and had at his mercy the captured Croesus, their fabulously rich king. When news was brought to him that the people of Sardis had rebelled, it would have been easy for him to reduce them by force; but being unwilling either to sack such a fine city or to maintain an army there to police it, he thought of an unusual expedient for reducing it. He established in it brothels, taverns, and public games, and issued the proclamation that the inhabitants were to enjoy them. He found this type of garrison so effective that he never again had to draw the sword against the Lydians. These wretched people enjoyed themselves inventing all kinds of games, so that the Latins have derived the word from them, and what we call *pastimes* they call *ludi*, as if they meant to say *Lydi*. Not all tyrants have manifested so clearly their intention to effeminize their victims; but in fact, what the aforementioned despot publicly proclaimed and put into effect, most of the others have pursued secretly as an end. It is indeed the nature of the populace, whose density is always greater in the cities, to be suspicious toward one who has their welfare at heart, and gullible toward one who fools them. Do not imagine that there is any bird more easily caught by decoy, nor any fish sooner fixed on the hook by wormy bait, than are all these poor fools neatly tricked into servitude by the slightest feather passed, so to speak, before their mouths. Truly it is a marvelous thing that they let themselves be caught so quickly at the slightest tickling of their fancy. Plays, farces, spectacles, gladiators, strange beasts, medals, pictures, and other such opiates, these were for ancient peoples the bait toward slavery, the price of their liberty, the instruments of tyranny. By these practices and enticements the ancient dictators so successfully lulled their subjects under the yoke, that the stupefied peoples, fascinated by the pastimes and vain pleasures flashed before their eyes, learned subservience as naively, but not so creditably, as little children learn to read by looking at bright picture books. Roman tyrants invented a further refinement. They often provided the city wards with feasts to cajole the rabble, always more readily tempted by the pleasure of eating than by anything else. The most intelligent and understanding amongst them would not have quit his soup bowl to recover the liberty of the Republic of Plato. Tyrants would distribute largess, a bushel of wheat, a gallon of wine, and a sesterce: and then everybody would shamelessly cry, "Long live the King!" The fools did not realize that they were merely recovering a portion of their own property, and that their ruler could not have given them what they were receiving without having first taken it from them. A man might one day be presented with a sesterce and gorge himself at the public feast, lauding Tiberius and Nero for handsome liberality, who on the morrow, would be forced to abandon his property to their avarice, his children to their lust, his very blood to the cruelty of these magnificent emperors, without offering any more resistance than a stone or a tree stump. The mob has always behaved in this way---eagerly open to bribes that cannot be honorably accepted, and dissolutely callous to degradation and insult that cannot be honorably endured. Nowadays I do not meet anyone who, on hearing mention of Nero, does not shudder at the very name of that hideous monster, that disgusting and vile pestilence. Yet when he died---when this incendiary, this executioner, this savage beast, died as vilely as he had lived---the noble Roman people, mindful of his games and his festivals, were saddened to the point of wearing mourning for him. Thus wrote Cornelius Tacitus, a competent and serious author, and one of the most reliable. This will not be considered peculiar in view of what this same people had previously done at the death of Julius Caesar, who had swept away their laws and their liberty, in whose character, it seems to me, there was nothing worth while, for his very liberality, which is so highly praised, was more baneful than the cruelest tyrant who ever existed, because it was actually this poisonous amiability of his that sweetened servitude for the Roman people. After his death, that people, still preserving on their palates the flavor of his banquets and in their minds the memory of his prodigality, vied with one another to pay him homage. They piled up the seats of the Forum for the great fire that reduced his body to ashes, and later raised a column to him as to "The Father of His People." (Such was the inscription on the capital.) They did him more honor, dead as he was, than they had any right to confer upon any man in the world, except perhaps on those who had killed him..

They didn't even neglect, these Roman emperors, to assume generally the title of Tribune of the People, partly because this office was held sacred and inviolable and also because it had been founded for the defense and protection of the people and enjoyed the favor of the state. By this means they made sure that the populace would trust them completely, as if they merely used the title and did not abuse it. Today there are some who do not behave very differently; they never undertake an unjust policy, even one of some importance, without prefacing it with some pretty speech concerning public welfare and common good. You well know, O Longa, this formula which they use quite cleverly in certain places; although for the most part, to be sure, there cannot be cleverness where there is so much impudence. The kings of the Assyrians and even after them those of the Medes showed themselves in public as seldom as possible in order to set up a doubt in the minds of the rabble as to whether they were not in some way more than man, and thereby to encourage people to use their imagination for those things which they cannot judge by sight. Thus a great many nations who for a long time dwelt under the control of the Assyrians became accustomed, with all this mystery, to their own subjection, and submitted the more readily for not knowing what sort of master they had, or scarcely even if they had one, all of them fearing by report someone they had never seen. The earliest kings of Egypt rarely showed themselves without carrying a cat, or sometimes a branch, or appearing with fire on their heads, masking themselves with these objects and parading like workers of magic. By doing this they inspired their subjects with reverence and admiration, whereas with people neither too stupid nor too slavish they would merely have aroused, it seems to me, amusement and laughter. It is pitiful to review the list of devices that early despots used to establish their tyranny; to discover how many little tricks they employed, always finding the populace conveniently gullible, readily caught in the net as soon as it was spread. Indeed they always fooled their victims so easily that while mocking them they enslaved them the more.

What comment can I make concerning another fine counterfeit that ancient peoples accepted as true money? They believed firmly that the great toe of Pyrrhus, king of Epirus, performed miracles and cured diseases of the spleen; they even enhanced the tale further with the legend that this toe, after the corpse had been burned, was found among the ashes, untouched by the fire. In this wise a foolish people itself invents lies and then believes them. Many men have recounted such things, but in such a way that it is easy to see that the parts were pieced together from idle gossip of the city and silly reports from the rabble. When Vespasian, returning from Assyria, passes through Alexandria on his way to Rome to take possession of the empire, he performs wonders: he makes the crippled straight, restores sight to the blind, and does many other fine things, concerning which the credulous and undiscriminating were, in my opinion, more blind than those cured. Tyrants themselves have wondered that men could endure the persecution of a single man; they have insisted on using religion for their own protection and, where possible, have borrowed a stray bit of divinity to bolster up their evil ways. If we are to believe the Sybil of Virgil, Salmoneus, in torment for having paraded as Jupiter in order to deceive the populace, now atones in nethermost Hell:

> He suffered endless torment for having dared to
>   imitate
> The thunderbolts of heaven and the flames of
>   Jupiter.
> Upon a chariot drawn by four chargers he went,
>   unsteadily
> Riding aloft, in his fist a great shining torch.
> Among the Greeks and into the market-place
> In the heart of the city of Elis he had ridden
>   boldly:
> And displaying thus his vainglory he assumed
> An honor which undeniably belongs to the gods
>   alone.
> This fool who imitated storm and the inimitable
>   thunderbolt
> By clash of brass and with his dizzying charge
> On horn-hoofed steeds, the all-powerful Father
>   beheld,
> Hurled not a torch, nor the feeble light
> From a waxen taper with its smoky fumes,
> But by the furious blast of thunder and lightning

He brought him low, his heels above his head.

If such a one, who in his time acted merely through the folly of insolence, is so well received in Hell, I think that those who have used religion as a cloak to hide their vileness will be even more deservedly lodged in the same place..

Our own leaders have employed in France certain similar devices, such as toads, fleurs-de-lys, sacred vessels, and standards with flames of gold. However that may be, I do not wish, for my part, to be incredulous, since neither we nor our ancestors have had any occasion up to now for skepticism. Our kings have always been so generous in times of peace and so valiant in time of war, that from birth they seem not to have been created by nature like many others, but even before birth to have been designated by Almighty God for the government and preservation of this kingdom. Even if this were not so, yet should I not enter the tilting ground to call in question the truth of our traditions, or to examine them so strictly as to take away their fine conceits. Here is such a field for our French poetry, now not merely honored but, it seems to me, reborn through our Rosnard, our Baif, our Bellay. These poets are defending our language so well that I dare to believe that very soon neither the Greeks nor the Latins will in this respect have any advantage over us except possibly that of seniority. And I should assuredly do wrong to our poesy---I like to use that word despite the fact that several have rhymed mechanically, for I still discern a number of men today capable of ennobling poetry and restoring it to its first lustre---but, as I say, I should do the Muse great injury if I deprived her now of those fine tales about. King Clovis, amongst which it seems to me I can already see how agreeably and how happily the inspiration of our Ronsard in his Frunciade will play. I appreciate his loftiness, I am aware of his keen spirit, and I know the charm of the man: he will appropriate the oriflamme to his use much as did the Romans their sacred bucklers and the shields cast from heaven to earth, according to Virgil. He will use our phial of holy oil much as the Athenians used the basket of Ericthonius; he will win applause for our deeds of valor as they did for their olive wreath which they insist can still be found in Minerva's tower. Certainly I should be presumptuous if I tried to cast slurs on our records and thus invade the realm of our poets.

But to return to our subject, the thread of which I have unwittingly lost in this discussion: it has always happened that tyrants, in order to strengthen their power, have made every effort to train their people not only in obedience and servility toward themselves, but also in adoration. Therefore all that I have said up to the present concerning the means by which a more willing submission has been obtained applies to dictators in their relationship with the inferior and common classes.

(Part III)

I COME NOW to a point which is, in my opinion, the mainspring and the secret of domination, the support and foundation of tyranny. Whoever thinks that halberds, sentries, the placing of the watch, serve to protect and shield tyrants is, in my judgment, completely mistaken. These are used, it seems to me, more for ceremony and a show of force than for any reliance placed in them. The archers forbid the entrance to the palace to the poorly dressed who have no weapons, not to the well armed who can carry out some plot. Certainly it is easy to say of the Roman emperors that fewer escaped from danger by aid of their guards than were killed by their own archers.[18] It is not the troops on horseback, it is not the companies afoot, it is not arms that defend the tyrant. This does not seem credible on first thought, but it is nevertheless true that there are only four or five who maintain the dictator, four or five who keep the country in bondage to him. Five or six have always had access to his ear, and have either gone to him of their own accord, or else have been summoned by him, to be accomplices in his cruelties, companions in his pleausres, panders to his lusts, and sharers in his plunders. These six manage their chief so successfully that he

---

[18] Almost a third of the Roman Emperors were killed by their own soldiers. ---*M.N.R.*

71

comes to be held accountable not only for his own misdeeds but even for theirs. The six have six hundred who profit under them, and with the six hundred they do what they have accomplished with their tyrant. The six hundred maintain under them six thousand, whom they promote in rank, upon whom they confer the government of provinces or the direction of finances, in order that they may serve as instruments of avarice and cruelty, executing orders at the proper time and working such havoc all around that they could not last except under the shadow of the six hundred, nor be exempt from law and punishment except through their influence.

The consequence of all this is fatal indeed. And whoever is pleased to unwind the skein will observe that not the six thousand but a hundred thousand, and even millions, cling to the tyrant by this cord to which they are tied. According to Homer, Jupiter boasts of being able to draw to himself all the gods when he pulls a chain. Such a scheme caused the increase in the senate under Julius, the formation of new ranks, the creation of offices; not really, if properly considered, to reform justice, but to provide new supporters of despotism. In short, when the point is reached, through big favors or little ones, that large profits or small are obtained under a tyrant, there are found almost as many people to whom tyranny seems advantageous as those to whom liberty would seem desirable. Doctors declare that if, when some part of the body has gangrene a disturbance arises in another spot, it immediately flows to the troubled part. Even so, whenever a ruler makes himself a dictator, all the wicked dregs of the nation---I do not mean the pack of petty thieves and earless ruffians[19] who, in a republic, are unimportant in evil or good---but all those who are corrupted by burning ambition or

[19] The cutting off of ears as a punishment for thievery is very ancient. In the middle ages it was still practiced under St. Louis. Men so mutilated were dishonored and could not enter the clergy or the magistracy.---*H.K.*

extraordinary avarice, these gather around him and support him in order to have a share in the booty and to constitute themselves petty chiefs under the big tyrant. This is the practice among notorious robbers and famous pirates: some scour the country, others pursue voyagers; some lie in ambush, others keep a lookout; some commit murder, others robbery; and although there are among them differences in rank, some being only underlings while others are chieftains of gangs, yet is there not a single one among them who does not feel himself to be a sharer, if not of the main booty, at least in the pursuit of it. It is dependably related that Sicilian pirates gathered in such great numbers that it became necessary to send against them Pompey the Great, and that they drew into their alliance fine towns and great cities in whose harbors they took refuge on returning from their expeditions, paying handsomely for the haven given their stolen goods..

Thus the despot subdues his subjects, some of them by means of others, and thus is he protected by those from whom, if they were decent men, he would have to guard himself; just as, in order to split wood, one has to use a wedge of the wood itself. Such are his archers, his guards, his halberdiers; not that they themselves do not suffer occasionally at his hands, but this riff-raff, abandoned alike by God and man, can be led to endure evil if permitted to commit it, not against him who exploits them, but against those who like themselves submit, but are helpless. Nevertheless, observing those men who painfully serve the tyrant in order to win some profit from his tyranny and from the subjection of the populace, I am often overcome with amazement at their wickedness and sometimes by pity for their folly. For, in all honesty, can it be in any way except in folly that you approach a tyrant, withdrawing further from your liberty and, so to speak, embracing with both hands your servitude? Let such men lay aside briefly their ambition, or let them forget for a moment their avarice, and look at themselves as they really are.

Then they will realize clearly that the townspeople, the peasants whom they trample under foot and treat worse than convicts or slaves, they will realize, I say, that these people, mistreated as they may be, are nevertheless, in comparison with themselves, better off and fairly free. The tiller of the soil and the artisan, no matter how enslaved, discharge their obligation when they do what they are told to do; but the dictator sees men about him wooing and begging his favor, and doing much more than he tells them to do. Such men must not only obey orders; they must anticipate his wishes; to satisfy him they must foresee his desires; they must wear themselves out, torment themselves, kill themselves with work in his interest, and accept his pleasure as their own, neglecting their preference for his, distorting their character and corrupting their nature; they must pay heed to his words, to his intonation, to his gestures, and to his glance. Let them have no eye, nor foot, nor hand that is not alert to respond to his wishes or to seek out his thoughts.

.Can that be called a happy life? Can it be called living? Is there anything more intolerable than that situation, I won't say for a man of mettle nor even for a man of high birth, but simply for a man of common sense or, to go even further, for anyone having the face of a man? What condition is more wretched than to live thus, with nothing to call one's own, receiving from someone else one's sustenance, one's power to act, one's body, one's very life?

.Still men accept servility in order to acquire wealth; as if they could acquire anything of their own when they cannot even assert that they belong to themselves, or as if anyone could possess under a tyrant a single thing in his own name. Yet they act as if their wealth really belonged to them, and forget that it is they themselves who give the ruler the power to deprive everybody of everything, leaving nothing that anyone can identify as belonging to somebody. They notice that nothing makes men so subservient to a tyrant's cruelty as property; that the possession of wealth is the worst of crimes against him, punishable even by death; that he loves nothing quite so much as money and ruins only the rich, who come before him as before a butcher, offering themselves so stuffed and bulging that they make his mouth water. These favorites should not recall so much the memory of those who have won great wealth from tyrants as of those who, after they had for some time amassed it, have lost to him their property as well as their lives; they should consider not how many others have gained a fortune, but rather how few of them have kept it. Whether we examine ancient history or simply the times in which we live, we shall see clearly how great is the number of those who, having by shameful means won the ear of princes---who either profit from their villainies or take advantage of their naiveté---were in the end reduced to nothing by these very princes; and although at first such servitors were met by a ready willingness to promote their interests, they later found an equally obvious inconstancy which brought them to ruin. Certainly among so large a number of people who have at one time or another had some relationship with bad rulers, there have been few or practically none at all who have not felt applied to themselves the tyrant's animosity, which they had formerly stirred up against others. Most often, after becoming rich by despoiling others, under the favor of his protection, they find themselves at last enriching him with their own spoils.

Even men of character---if it sometimes happens that a tyrant likes such a man well enough to hold him in his good graces, because in him shine forth the virtue and integrity that inspire a certain reverence even in the most depraved--even men of character, I say, could not long avoid succumbing to the common malady and would early experience the effects of tyranny at their own expense. A Seneca, a Burrus, a Thrasea, this triumverate of splendid men, will provide a sufficient reminder of such misfortune. Two of them were close to the tyrant by the fatal responsibility of holding in their hands the management of his

75

affairs, and both were esteemed and beloved by him. One of them, moreover, had a peculiar claim upon his friendship, having instructed his master as a child. Yet these three by their cruel death give sufficient evidence of how little faith one can place in the friendship of an evil ruler. Indeed what friendship may be expected from one whose heart is bitter enough to hate even his own people, who do naught else but obey him? It is because he does not know how to love that he ultimately impoverishes his own spirit and destroys his own empire.

Now if one would argue that these men fell into disgrace because they wanted to act honorably, let him look around boldly at others close to that same tyrant, and he will see that those who came into his favor and maintained themselves by dishonorable means did not fare much better. Who has ever heard tell of a love more centered, of an affection more persistent, who has ever read of a man more desperately attached to a woman than Nero was to Poppaea? Yet she was later poisoned by his own hand. Agrippina his mother had killed her husband, Claudius, in order to exalt her son; to gratify him she had never hesitated at doing or bearing anything; and yet this very son, her offspring, her emperor, elevated by her hand, after failing her often, finally took her life. It is indeed true that no one denies she would have well deserved this punishment, if only it had come to her by some other hand than that of the son she had brought into the world. Who was ever more easily managed, more naive, or, to speak quite frankly, a greater simpleton, than Claudius the Emperor? Who was ever more wrapped up in his wife than he in Messalina, whom he delivered finally into the hands of the executioner? Stupidity in a tyrant always renders him incapable of benevolent action; but in some mysterious way by dint of acting cruelly even towards those who are his closest associates, he seems to manifest what little intelligence he may have.

Quite generally known is the striking phrase of that other tyrant who, gazing at the throat of his wife, a woman he dearly loved and without whom it seemed he could not live, caressed her with this charming comment: "This lovely throat would be cut at once if I but gave the order." That is why the majority of the dictators of former days were commonly slain by their closest favorites who, observing the nature of tyranny, could not be so confident of the whim of the tyrant as they were distrustful of his power. Thus was Domitian killed by Stephen, Commodus by one of his mistresses, Antoninus by Macrinus, and practically all the others in similar violent fashion..

The fact is that the tyrant is never truly loved, nor does he love. Friendship is a sacred word, a holy thing; it is never developed except between persons of character, and never takes root except through mutual respect; it flourishes not so much by kindnesses as by sincerity. What makes one friend sure of another is the knowledge of his integrity: as guarantees he has his friend's fine nature, his honor, and his constancy. There can be no friendship where there is cruelty, where there is disloyalty, where there is injustice. And in places where the wicked gather there is conspiracy only, not companionship: these have no affection for one another; fear alone holds them together; they are not friends, they are merely accomplices.

Although it might not be impossible, yet it would be difficult to find true friendship in a tyrant; elevated above others and having no companions, he finds himself already beyond the pale of friendship, which receives its real sustenance from an equality that, to proceed without a limp, must have its two limbs equal. That is why there is honor among thieves (or so it is reported) in the sharing of the booty; they are peers and comrades; if they are not fond of one another they at least respect one another and do not seek to lessen their strength by squabbling. But the favorites of a tyrant can never feel entirely secure, and the less so because he has learned from them that he is all powerful and unlimited by any law or obligation. Thus it becomes his wont to consider his own will as reason enough, and to be master of all with never a compeer. Therefore it seems a pity that with so many examples at hand, with the danger always present, no one is anxious to act the wise man at the expense of the others, and that among so many persons fawning upon their ruler there is not a single one who has the wisdom and the boldness to say to him what, according to the fable,[20] the fox said to the lion who feigned illness: "I should be glad to enter your lair to pay my respects; but I see many tracks of beasts that have gone toward you, yet not a single trace of any who have come back."

These wretches see the glint of the despot's treasures and are bedazzled by the radiance of his splendor. Drawn by this brilliance they come near, without realizing they are approaching a flame that cannot fail to scorch them. Similarly attracted, the indiscreet satyr of the old fables, on seeing the bright fire brought down by Prometheus, found it so beautiful that he went and kissed it, and was burned[21]; so, as the Tuscan[22] poet reminds us, the moth, intent upon desire, seeks the flame because it shines, and also experiences its other quality, the burning. Moreover, even admitting that favorites may at times escape from the hands of him they serve, they are never safe from the ruler who comes after him. If he is good, they must render an account of their past and recognize at last that justice exists; if he is bad and resembles their late master, he will certainly have his own favorites, who are not usually satisfied to occupy in their turn merely the posts of their precedessors, but will more often insist on their wealth and their lives. Can anyone be found, then, who under such perilous circumstances and with so little security

---

[20] By Aesop.---*M.N.R.*

[21] Aeschylus' *Prometheus the Firebearer* (fragment).---*M.N.R.*

[22] Petrarch, *Cazoniere*, Sonnet XVII. La Boetie has accurately rendered the lines concerning the moth.---*H.K.*

will still be ambitious to fill such an ill-fated position and serve, despite such perils, so dangerous a master? Good God, what suffering, what martyrdom all this involves! To be occupied night and day in planning to please one person, and yet to fear him more than anyone else in the world; to be always on the watch, ears open, wondering whence the blow will come; to search out conspiracy, to be on guard against snares, to scan the faces of companions for signs of treachery, to smile at everybody and be mortally afraid of all, to be sure of nobody, either as an open enemy or as a reliable friend; showing always a gay countenance despite an apprehensive heart, unable to be joyous yet not daring to be sad!

However, there is satisfaction in examining what they get out of all this torment, what advantage they derive from all the trouble of their wretched existence. Actually the people never blame the tyrant for the evils they suffer, but they do place responsibility on those who influence him; peoples, nations, all compete with one another, even the peasants, even the tillers of the soil, in mentioning the names of the favorites, in analyzing their vices, and heaping upon them a thousand insults, a thousand obscenities, a thousand maledictions. All their prayers, all their vows are directed against these persons; they hold them accountable for all their misfortunes, their pestilences, their famines; and if at times they show them outward respect, at those very moments they are fuming in their hearts and hold them in greater horror than wild beasts. This is the glory and honor heaped upon influential favorites for their services by people who, if they could tear apart their living bodies, would still clamor for more, only half satiated by the agony they might behold. For even when the favorites are dead those who live after are never too lazy to blacken the names of these man-eaters[23]

---

[23] The word was used by Homer in the *Iliad*, Book I, Line 341.---*M.N.R.*

with the ink of a thousand pens, tear their reputations into bits in a thousand books, and drag, so to speak, their bones past posterity, forever punishing them after their death for their wicked lives.

Let us therefore learn while there is yet time, let us learn to do good. Let us raise our eyes to Heaven for the sake of our honor, for the very love of virtue, or, to speak wisely, for the love and praise of God Almighty, who is the infallible witness of our deeds and the just judge of our faults. As for me, I truly believe I am right, since there is nothing so contrary to a generous and loving God as tyranny---I believe He has reserved, in a separate spot in Hell, some very special punishment for tyrants and their accomplices.